'Nathalie Lugand skilfully crosses two traditionally separate fields of study – work and sexuality – and transforms our perspective on desire. This book is provocative, bold and out of the box. A must read.'

Pascale Molinier, *Professor of Social Psychology, University Sorbonne Paris Nord, France*

A PSYCHODYNAMIC APPROACH TO FEMALE DOMINATION IN BDSM RELATIONSHIPS

This ground-breaking book explores contemporary forms of BDSM where women dominate in relationships and professions, opening new paths for psychological research in commercial and non-commercial BDSM.

Based on a unique combination of qualitative investigation and academic research, it examines how BDSM has often crystalized conflicts in contemporary feminist debates, where sexually dominant women are pictured either as victims or as agents of resistance to the patriarchy. Nathalie Lugand argues that female domination in heterosexual BDSM is above all situated in a continuum structured by the values of care and by the circulation of money. Through a novel psychodynamic approach, Lugand demystifies BDSM relationships where women dominate, considering the impact of social relations of work in the construction of sexual identity and analyzing the difficulties that they cause in the erotic economy. The book affirms that to better understand the pleasure taken in female domination practices and the difficulties for women to impose themselves as dominatrixes, it is necessary to shift the focus away from transgressive aspects and look towards the workplace and the organization of work in women's sexuality.

Using field immersion to comprehensively investigate the blurred boundaries between life and work in the BDSM community, *A Psychodynamic Approach to Female Domination in BDSM Relationships* provides the opportunity for a new interpretation of sexuality, overturning the existing theoretical frameworks used in clinical psychology and psychoanalysis. This book is essential reading for researchers and academics in psychology, gender studies, political and social sciences, and human sexuality, as well as activists defending the human rights of sex workers around the world.

Nathalie Lugand is a member of the research laboratory UTRPP (transversal unity of psychogenesis and psychopathology) at the University Sorbonne Paris Nord. Her work focuses on the relationship between gender, sexuality, work, and mental health.

A PSYCHODYNAMIC APPROACH TO FEMALE DOMINATION IN BDSM RELATIONSHIPS

Sexuality Between Pleasure and Work

Nathalie Lugand

Routledge
Taylor & Francis Group

LONDON AND NEW YORK

Designed cover image: © Getty Images

First published 2023
by Routledge
4 Park Square, Milton Park, Abingdon, Oxon OX14 4RN

and by Routledge
605 Third Avenue, New York, NY 10158

Routledge is an imprint of the Taylor & Francis Group, an informa business

British Library Cataloguing-in-Publication Data
A catalogue record for this book is available from the British Library

Library of Congress Cataloging-in-Publication Data
Names: Lugand, Nathalie, author.
Title: A psychodynamic approach to female domination in BDSM
relationships: sexuality between pleasure and work / Nathalie Lugand.
Description: Abingdon, Oxon ; New York, NY : Routledge, 2023. |
Includes bibliographical references and index. | Identifiers: LCCN
2022030819 (print) | LCCN 2022030820 (ebook) |
ISBN 9781032192925 (paperback) | ISBN 9781032192956 (hardback) |
ISBN 9781003258537 (ebook)
Subjects: LCSH: Sexual dominance and submission. | Women—Sexual
behavior. | Sex.
Classification: LCC HQ79 .L85 2023 (print) | LCC HQ79 (ebook) |
DDC 306.7082—dc23/eng/20220815
LC record available at https://lccn.loc.gov/2022030819
LC ebook record available at https://lccn.loc.gov/2022030820

ISBN: 9781032192956 (hbk)
ISBN: 9781032192925 (pbk)
ISBN: 9781003258537 (ebk)

DOI: 10.4324/9781003258537

Typeset in Bembo
by codeMantra

CONTENTS

INTRODUCTION

1 Psychological framework

I met Tracy while I was busy writing this book. I learned that she was a professional dominatrix in the 1990s in New York. Not without a touch of melancholy, Tracy talks about the BDSM[1] scene in the US and the meetings she had with other women who trained her as a professional dominatrix and transformed her as a person. She complains about the lack of sensuality of the Berlin scene, where the organization and supervision of workshops and Stammtisch[2] that remind her of management techniques found everywhere in the service sector. Nothing is very sexy. She doesn't feel the spontaneity, the freshness, the enthusiasm, and the sensuality that she experienced on the New York scene. This overlaps with what Gail Rubin discusses in a different context. In a speech held at the Journey man II Academy ceremony on October 4, 1997, she spoke with regret about the commercial exploitation of BDSM that appeared in the 1980s at public parties.

> Before, many parties were informal rituals of solidarity, pleasure, celebration and bonding. ... Even in recreational games the focus was on the quality of the connection between the players and the sharing and building of energy where everyone in the space could "glide" together .... The scene now has become more fashionable, popular rather than stigmatized and inspiring contempt.[3]

I remained skeptical of the "it was better before" that these words echo and the melancholy song of the participants of the older generation. That said, it is equally important to consider the role of societal changes on sexuality and to take seriously the fact that sexuality is sensitive to variations in societies and cultures. The changes introduced by the education and emancipation of women,

DOI: 10.4324/9781003258537-1

by their access to a profession, a salary, and autonomy, have created the possibility of recreational sex for them and therefore of seeing an increase in the number of women engaged in BDSM practices. It is therefore necessary to take seriously the effects of the organization of work on sexualities.

How do we transform ourselves through work? What difficulties does the sexual division of labor cause in the erotic economy? How does work turn out to be both a formative and a self-transformative movement? What are the effects of the organization of work on the construction of sexual identity? What does the reference to ethics in BDSM relations bring to the practices of female domination? In what way and how do the defenses developed by women and men take hold in intimate life? What are the impacts of recent changes in the organization of work on the modalities of female domination?

Why write a book on female domination focused on the notion of work? This notion is already highlighted in Lindemann's book (Lindemann 2012: 30), which is an ethnographic study of professional dominatrixes. That said, we do not work with the same definition of work, and that makes all the difference. In her book, the notion of work is synonymous with salaried employment. This means that non-professional practices are not addressed. The definition of the work I deal with is broader. It is not limited to a restricted conception of male wage-earning but includes domestic work in the category of work. It deconstructs the opposition between active and inactive, work and non-work, paid and unpaid work, and work and unemployment. Moreover, I consider the work of female domination participants realized in the professional and domestic spheres, and also the reflective work conducted upon sexual desires, sexual practices, and sexual fantasies.[4]

In fact, the purpose of this book is to propose an analysis of the relations of female domination that considers the work in the productive and material sphere as well as the psyche. It gives an account of the dynamics of the mobilization of intelligence and the personality in the practices of female domination. I am not only taking into account both commercial and non-commercial BDSM but also the intra- and intersubjective dynamics at play in the relations between the two. The theoretical framework – the psychodynamics of work – upon which this book is based provides an ideal opportunity to show how the separation usually made between the two types of exchange is erroneous, if not a "sting."[5]

The psychodynamic analysis of work associated primarily with Christophe Dejours emerged as a field in France in the 1950s. It focuses on the issue of suffering at work. The etymology of the term *work* is in Latin "tripalium": instrument of torture. Work is originally an instrument of torture and therefore by definition a generator of suffering. Until the classical era, the word *work* expressed ideas of fatigue, pain, torment, displeasure, shame, boredom, feelings of injustice, and painful obligation. If men and women continuously experienced these sufferings caused by work, they simply could not work. No one would spend their day cleaning hotel rooms in painful positions, would not take orders from their superiors, and would not accompany people who are considered difficult or violent. In the psychodynamics of work, if suffering is recognized as an individual experience, the attention is focused on the fight against suffering at work, which can sometimes involve rules of cooperation and defense. The existence of collectively developed and sustained defensive strategies is the most surprising empirical discovery of work psychodynamics (Dejours 1993). These defense strategies constructed collectively by the workers bear the specific mark of the constraints inherent in each work situation.

The analysis is considered "dynamic" in the sense that it studies the conflicts that arise from the encounter between the individual and work situations. The psychodynamics of work identifies the intra- and intersubjective dynamics at play in the social relationships that workers have with their work. It thus promotes the understanding of the attitudes of the individual in a work situation. This idea is fundamental to understanding the relationship between subjectivity and working. Working is to mobilize one's body, one's intelligence, and one's person for a production that has use value (Dejours 2016: 221). Thus, subjectivation through work is not a privilege confined to the traditional forms of the arts and crafts. One can only work by engaging one's subjectivity. It is because of this investment that work is a fundamental vector of both self-fulfillment and, when it goes wrong, of painful experiences that can go as far as destabilizing one's health. What the clinic of work brings to everyday life is indeed, today as in the past, that the subjective engagement in work goes beyond the necessity of "earning a living," and the question of recognition, as conceived by the psychodynamics of work, is indeed closely linked to that of identity.

One of the key ideas of the psychodynamics of work is the idea that "real" work often remains invisible. According to Dejours,

> Work is the coordinated activity deployed by men and women to cope with what, in a utilitarian task, cannot be obtained by the strict execution of the prescribed organization: know-how, division of labor, rules, and technical skills. To work consists in exercising one's intelligence in order to "fill the gap between the prescribed work and actual work (the real of work)" (Dejours 2009 V2: 20) and to find an answer and to give a sense to this primitive suffering. "Work is, in this sense, enigmatic, since the investments made by individuals in their work may be expressed in drives and forms of sublimation of which they are not consciously aware."
>
> *(Marks 2019: 1)*

Thus, starting from the idea that work is not simply an affair of the material sphere but also, above all, an affair of the psyche, I show that it supposes a commitment of oneself where the body plays a fundamental role. Intuition, bad feeling, impression of déjà vu, sensation of belly, sharp look, the intelligence of the body is not explained itself, but it arises abruptly, in the moment, the unexpected, everywhere where the mechanical and technological order does not function (Molinier 2000). The work reveals that it is in the body itself that the subject invests the world to make it his own and to inhabit it. The body of which I speak here is called, in psychoanalysis, "the erogenous body" (Dejours 2009 V1: 185). This body is not given at birth but is built progressively in the relationship of body to body between the child and the adult around the care of the body, which is contaminated by the sexual body.

Thus, admitting the legitimacy of a revaluation of the notion of work inevitably leads to the sensitive question of the relationship between work and sexuality. Work is considered central to the development of personality from infancy to maturity. The psychodynamics of work considers the impact of the social relations of work in the construction of the sexual identity and analyzes the difficulties they involve in the erotic economy. The role of the work in the dynamics of the psychic and social process makes the classic separation between work and sexuality invalid. "Psychic functioning is not divisible" (Dejours 2015: 281).

2 BDSM as a social behavior

In this book, I assume that sexuality is not only a private, intimate, natural matter, but it also depends on the social and historical contexts in which these sexualities take shape. And, therefore, we are not born dominant or submissive, but we become it. It is a complete reversal of the traditional theses of psychoanalysis, which considers that the sexual is endowed with a complete autonomy with regard to the social.

This work is not intended to help identify the distinctive signs of *naturally* dominant women, as I am sometimes asked by submissive men. I consider female domination as a set of desires, sexual fantasies, and signifying practices situated culturally and historically. On the contrary, I am interested in these essentialist ideas because they hold an important place in the erotic economy of BDSM practitioners, starting with the books on the subject. When I began my dissertation, I explored the literature on sadism and masochism, and it became apparent that psychology and psychoanalysis provided a preponderant and even hegemonic work on these "sexual aberrations" until the 1980s. Until then, the idea of the naturalness of masochism and sadism was radical. When in 1897, Havelock Ellis, for example, provided more information on the subject and put forward the hypothesis of an instinctual drive linking the affects of pain and pleasure, he was referring to the biological body in the strict sense.

The terms *masochism* and *sadism* were coined by Krafft-Ebing in 1890. He introduced them the following year in the sixth edition of *Psychopathia Sexualis* (1891). The word *sadism* is derived from the name of the decried Marquis de Sade, whose obscene novels are full of sensuality and cruelty. The word *masochism* is derived from the name of the writer Sacher-Masoch, who frequently described the connection of voluptuousness with submission to cruelties. Defining sadism as the experience of sexual sensations of pleasure (including orgasm) produced by acts of cruelty and corporal punishment afflicted on a person, Krafft-Ebing considers sadism as a deep desire to humiliate, hurt, make suffer, and see destruction of others with the intention to create sexual pleasure. As for masochism, it would be based on the desire to be completely controlled and subjected to the desire of the other, and to be treated by this person as by a master, abused and humiliated.

A turning point was taken in the 1980s when theorists of these sexualities revealed the cooperation, interdependence, trust, and care at work between the two partners in these relationships. Some pioneering authors from the 1990s onward, such as Charles Moser and J. J. Madeson (2002), Jay Wiseman (1996), and Phillip Miller and Molly Devon (1995), attempted to explain sadistic and masochistic experiences from a non-psychopathological point of view by considering them as a form of social behavior. Their conception of sexuality and the body that experiences it gives an essential place to subjectivity. Since then, many other authors have also focused their analyses on the interactions between participants of BDSM practices within their subcultures. All of these authors related to BDSM communities place a central emphasis on empathy and think of BDSM relationships in terms of interdependence. It is a matter of caring about someone (caring about), taking care of someone (caring), and being the object of care (care receiving). BDSM is thus presented as a practice in which care for the other and responsibility are exercised and realized.

The work of these authors is inseparable from the history of BDSM and the American leather communities. These communities developed most notably through the cultural history of the Bay Area in San Francisco, where the avant-garde leather scene from the 1950s to the 1970s was born (Weiss 2011). These are communities of men who returned to the US after World War II and settled in cities such as San Francisco, Los Angeles, and New York, where they created, as early as the 1950s, the first social meeting spaces dedicated to leather sexualities. Leathermen have their own sexuality and lifestyle based on leather and denim, which is a brutal, often kinky sexuality. They adopt, according to D. L. Boisvert, a code of ethics that translates military values of loyalty, responsibility, honor, and trust into a personal ethic to forge deep human relationships. This is related to the BDSM "Safe, Sane, Consensual" ethic. This ethic, born in the 1980s in the US in the gay BDSM community, has circulated within the BDSM communities and has become a common ethic in all BDSM circles. It tends to draw a line between what is clearly defensible, in terms of both social structures and personal well-being, and what is indefensible, or at least highly questionable (Lugand and Molinier 2017). Recently other approaches – namely, Risk Aware Consensual Kink (RACK), 4Cs (Caring, Communication, Consent, and Caution), and PRICK (Personal-Responsibility Informed Consensual Kink) – have also been used as a basic framework for structuring the negotiation of participation in BDSM (Williams et al. 2014) and helping to emphasize varying values that differentiate BDSM practices from abuse and violence.

3 Femininity and domination are not good couples?

During my readings on BDSM, I quickly realized that there were few texts dedicated to dominant women. The attention is always focused on the masochistic woman, which is explained in the first place by the approval of psychological analyses (Krafft-Ebing 1895; Deutsch 1998 [1948]; Horney 1967; Robertiello 1970) on masochism and its essentialist association with the nature of the woman. Masochism is conjugated in the feminine and sadism in the masculine.

Dominant women are disturbing, a woman I interviewed told me. They disturb because they disrupt the superposition of the masculine/active and the feminine/passive. Indeed, Krafft-Ebing's thinking is based on a biological and heterosexual conception of sexuality. "The male must like to dominate, the female must like to submit: this is because the biology of procreation is anchored in the human soul" (Vandermeersch 2002: 224).

Here, it is the women who dominate the men. The acts are carried out on the men. They are those who direct the scene. The dominant women thus embody a criticism made to the centrality of the role played by the sexual difference in the Freudian theories. This explains why when the sadism of women is discussed, as is the case, for example, by the psychologist Magnus Hirschfeld (1935), sadism in women is considered a real abomination. He coined the concept of symbolic sadism in 1925 in *Sexual Anomalies and Perversions* to explain this sexual behavior which he defines in terms of sexual pathology. According to him, symbolic sadism is invariably totalitarian because the sadistic woman is dominant throughout and her sadism is the dominant factor in her professional, social, and sexual lives. On the other hand, the man is able to leave his sadism at home (Gosselin and Wilson 1980). So any woman who is active professionally or in her sexual life takes the risk of being labeled as abnormal.

Feminists focus their analysis on masochism and, in this sense, submit to the psychoanalytical precept that masochism is feminine (Hart 2003: 108). Thus, while a politics of care in contemporary theories has curbed the influence of definitions of sadomasochism described in terms of an abomination of nature, by neglecting dominant women, feminist studies contribute to their being seen as an exception – women who are more masculine than feminine – and thus stigmatize them.

The few studies on the subject present their sexual orientation in terms of "internalization of the violent patterns of domination/submission of the sexist patriarchy" (Linden et al. 1982) or of "masculinity complex" (Silverman 1992). The same logic is found at work in feminist anti-BDSM critiques, arguing that dominant women, to use Linda. Hart's phrase, have "internalized violent patterns of domination/submission of heterosexist patriarchy" and "[are] therefore unwitting victims who perpetuate patterns of oppression." This is also the point of view of Poutrain, in *Sexe et pouvoir*, for whom the female domination would only reproduce the patterns of the male domination (Poutrain 2003). Deleuze's analyses seem more positive at first glance. Indeed this last considers the capacities of resistance of the female domination to the gendered patriarchy. That said this dimension is put forward only in that it allows the production of a "new man" to the "gynarchist sensibilities" (Deleuze 1967). Mostly, in the analyses concerning the feminine domination in the BDSM relations, we see the difficulty to consider the possibility of a feminine thought subject, that is to say, a subject thought in an autonomous way and not subordinated in relation to the men and the masculine.

To explain that some people make a choice in sexual orientation that is judged atypical, without questioning the complementarity between the sexes, the notion of psychic bisexuality can be used as an adjustment variable. Everyone would have a feminine and a masculine part in himself or herself, with a different dosage according to the individuals. That would be a theoretical solution less stigmatizing for women than their interpretation of their sexual orientation in terms of phallic claims or masculinity complex and less openly homophobic toward masochistic men. "This interpretation, contrary to the interpretations mentioned above, responds to the criticisms formulated against a model of sexuality based on the opposition of man/active and woman/passive. It avoids, therefore, perceiving and categorizing active women (sexually, professionally, etc.) as 'masculine'" (Molinier 2006: 231).

4 Thinking female domination through the lens of work

If femininity and sexual domination appear as an epistemological monster, it is largely by virtue of the fact that psychological analyses have reinforced the cultural and historical link between passivity and femininity. They should accept their natural passivity and masochism in order to progress toward "the desire for a child" and to this end become more feminine and gentle, and fantasize about being underneath in sexual relations (Joseph 1965: 44–45). This link was previously solidified by the fact that the tasks of care, linked to empathy and concern for others, are in Western societies carried out mostly by women. De facto, this specifically "feminine" work is regularly confused with the register of "loving consent" and "maternal love," and it is confused with a feminine disposition that would be inherent to the psycho-cognitive development of women.

On the one hand, the association between care, love, and the nature of women can be seen as one of the main aspects that has prevented the care of people from being recognized as a legitimate form of work by bringing it into the private realm; on the other hand, this conceptual separation of care from the public realm can be seen as maintained by the fear of the mutual contamination of the intimate sphere and rational economic behaviors (Zelizer 2005). Seeing the public/private relationship only in terms of a dichotomy and not giving importance to the domestic sphere means neglecting not only the family but also the power relations existing within it. As Susan Moller Okin points out, mainstream political theorists thus ignore "the political nature of the family" and "the importance of justice in personal life" (1991: 71). One can only agree with these statements when one considers the fact that this divide maintains the boundary of these spheres by stigmatizing some women who do not conform to socially sanctioned gender norms as whores, particularly those who demand money in exchange for sex (Pheterson 1993).

Thinkers of BDSM sexuality such as Michelle Foucault and Gilles Deleuze understand BDSM sexualities as resistance to gender relations through the ability of these sexualities to invert power relations. But these theories – more concerned with the "pursuit of ecstasy" that these sexualities promise and their "political salvation" – have tended to deny the continuity between the political structure of oppression and sexuality (Bersani 1995). Thus, they do not allow us to think and undo the association between the passive nature of women and the devalued work of care.

Is female domination the cardinal form of the subversion of social gender relations? Or is it necessary that the social relations of sex have been previously subverted for a relation following the criteria of consensual to occur? How do masochistic men manage to respect dominant women despite the social system of sex and the whore stigma? How is it possible that they don't just impose their fantasies on them like Sacher-Masoch imposed his on Wanda and don't always dispose of them as they would dispose of an "object"? What do they seek of their own subjectivity in the encounter with the dominant woman? What do they risk losing? How does what men and women do affect their sexual economy of bodies? How does the responsibility historically placed on women and "minority subjects" (Paperman and Molinier 2011: 190) translate into sexuality? How do the defenses developed to fight against the whore stigma manifest themselves in sexuality?

My book answers this question by articulating the stakes of the psychodynamics of work with those of gender studies based on the work of Dejours (1980/2000), Hirata and Kergoat (1988), and Molinier (2000, 2009). They have proposed concepts at the crossroads of two theoretical fields, namely, virility as a defensive ideology, associated with the exercise of risk or power occupations, and muliebrity, associated with the naturalization of feminine qualifications. Virility as a defense implies a set of behaviors in men that come back to deny their co-professional and psychic vulnerability, which is translated in their work by the denial of reality of the dimensions of the activity that make them suffer.

> The psychological spring of virility is the shame of passing for a woman. What is considered shameful, unworthy of a man, is to be unable to control the tender current of his emotions, to flee, to collapse in front of a difficult situation. What is exalted, solicited and exercised, it is the aggressiveness of the male and its concretization in the virile courage.
>
> *(Molinier 2000: 14)*

As for the muliebrity, it designates the alienation of the female subjectivity in the stereotypes of the socially constructed femininity and in the submission (Dejours 1988). The processes of "masquerade femininity" (in the sense of Joan Rivière) aiming to "make the woman" would have the goal of being accepted in a world dominated by the men, where the women would not know how to behave as their equals/similars, under penalty of reprisals, and/or to stop making them horny (Molinier 2020).

> The muliebrity covers what Nicole-Claude Mathieu (1991) designates under the term of dominated conscience but by giving it the psychological content of a defense against the chronic deficit of recognition of the female work. The muliebrity would be the defense mobilized by the women to support, in both senses of the term, the virility. Compulsive attitudes of cleanliness among housewives and nurses' aides, idealization of self-giving among nurses or of love for children among male early childhood professionals.
>
> *(Molinier 2000: 37)*

I articulate the reflections made in psychodynamics of work with those made in gender studies to bring forward the discussion opened by Danièle Kergoat and Helena Hirta on the idea that the struggle against suffering in the workplace pushes its ramifications into the intimacy of families and into the sexual life. There would be forms of defensive sexuality, deviances, or domestic violence, which would not be entirely explained by the reference to infantile neurosis. Thus, we can clinically identify a sort of defensive continuum between the struggle against suffering in the workplace and forms of "compulsive" or even "hygienic" sexuality, where the partner is reduced to the rank of an object, a female. Work appears as a crucial link in understanding the destinies of sexual life, between fornication and erotic experience. In this book, I show that when the social and ethical conditions of a creative work are not met, the defensive ideologies of gender invest even the psychic processes mobilized in the amorous meeting. I show how the fulfillment of the work that is seen in forms of developed sensibility operates in the construction of sexuality and sexual pleasure.

That being said, we live in a world where male domination has not been abolished. I will therefore also show how the dynamics of the submissive man/ dominant woman relationship in intimacy is marked by gender relations and thus obeys the injunction to conform to gender norms, regardless of the pleasure and fulfillment provided by the work.

Notes

1 BDSM is an amalgam of three acronyms: bondage and discipline (B/D), domination and submission (D/S), and sadomasochism (S/M). BDSM was previously known as sadomasochism (or S/M). In this book I refer to BDSM but I keep the terminology used by the theorists and BDSM participants in the citations.
2 Stammtisch: In Germany, group of people who gather at every now and then.
3 In Weiss (2011), p. 65.
4 Sexual fantasies are the scenarios of desire, initially shaped from the translation of parental sexual fantasies and then reworked, transformed, and enriched from new materials coming from the external world. de Lauretis (2007) shows that fantasies are thus constructed at the intersection between what is most singularized in the subject, his or her "private fantasies," and what is most culturally shared, the "public

fantasies" (the social representations of sexuality). Based on the work of Laplanche and Pontalis, de Lauretis grants to the fantasy a structuring role in the constitution of the sexual subject.

5 I refer to Paola Tabet who describes the distinction usually made between commercial sexuality and non-commercial sexuality as a "sting" (Tabet 2004).

Bibliography

Bersani L. (1995). *Homos: Repenser l'identité*. Paris, Odile Jacob.

Dejours C. (1980). Travail: usure mentale, Bayard, 3 ème éd. 2000.

Dejours C. (1988). Le masculin entre sexualité et société. *Adolescence*, 6(1), 89–116.

Dejours C. (1993). Coopération et construction de l'identité en situation de travail. Multitudes: Revue politique, artistique, philosophique: http://www.multitudes.net/Cooperation-et-construction-de-l/

Dejours C. (1996). Centralité du travail et théorie de la sexualité. *Adolescence*, 14(2), 9–29.

Dejours C. (1998). *Souffrance en France*. Paris, Seuil.

Dejours C. (2000). Différence anatomique et reconnaissance du réel dans le travail. *les Cahiers du Genre*, 29, 101–126.

Dejours C. (2009). *Travail vivant. 1: Sexualité et travail*. Paris, Petite Bibliotheque Payot.

Dejours C. (2015) 1993. *Travail: Usure mentale*. Paris, Bayard.

Dejours C. (2016) 1998. Chapitre IX. "Travailler n'est pas déroger". Dans: C. Dejours, *Situations du travail* (pp. 219–228). Paris cedex 14: Presses Universitaires de France.

De Lauretis T. (1994). *Practice of Love: Perverse Desire*. Bloomington and Indianapolis, Indiana University Press.

De Lauretis T. (2007). Théorie queer et culture populaires. De Foucault à Cronenberg. Paris, La dispute coll. "Le genre du monde," traduit par Marie-Hélène Bourcier.

Deleuze G. (1967). *Présentation de Sacher-Masoch, Le froid et le cruel*. Paris, Les éditions de minuit.

Deutsch H. (1998) 1948. *Psychologie der Frau*. Bern, Fachbuchhandlung für Psychologie.

Gosselin C., Wilson G. (1980). *Sexual Variations: Fetishism, Sadomasochism, and Transvestism*. New York, Simon and Schuster.

Hart L. (2003). *La performance sadomasochiste: Entre corps et chair*. Paris, EPEL.

Hirata H., Kergoat D. (1988). Rapports sociaux de sexe et psychopathologie du travail. In C. Dejours (dir.), *Plaisir et souffrance dans le travail*, Vol. 2, 131–176. Paris, Edition de l'AOCIP.

Hirschfeld M. (1935). *Sexual anomalies and perversions physical and psychological development and treatment: A textbook for students, psychologists, criminologists, probation officers, judges, and educationists*. Torch, London.

Horney K. (1967). The problem of the feminine masochism. In H. M. Ruitenbeek (Hrsg.), *The Psychotherapy of Perversion*. New York, Citadel Press.

Joseph E. D. (1965). *Beating Fantasies and Regressive Ego Phenomena in Psychoanalysis*. The Kris Study Group of the New York Psychoanalysis Institute. New York, International Universities Press.

Krafft-Ebing R. von (1983) 1895. *Psychopathia Sexualis*, trad. 8Eme éd. allemande, E. Laurent, S. Scapo, G. Carré, Paris, Carré.

Lindemann D. (2012). *Dominatrix: Gender, Eroticism, and Control in the Dungeon*. Chicago, IL, University of Chicago Press.

Linden R. R., Pagano D. R., Russell D. E. H., Star S. L. (1982). *Against Sadomasochism: A Radical Feminist Analysis*. California, Frog in the Well.

Lugand N., Molinier P. (2017). *Care et souci de soi dans les relations BDSM.* In M. Álvarez, I. Hekmat, S. Lauret (Eds.), *L'amour: création et société.* Paris, Michel Houdiard.

Marks J. (2019). The psychodynamic analysis of work. *Modern and Contemporary France,* 28(1), 1–17.

Mathieu N.-C. (1991). *L'anatomie politique. Catégorisations et idéologies du sexe.* Paris, Coll Recherches. Côté-femmes Editions.

Miller P., Devon M. (1995). *Screw the Roses, Send Me the Thorns: The Romance and Sexual Sorcery of Sadomasochism.* Fairfield, CT, Mystic Roses Books.

Molinier P. (2000). Virilité défensive, masculinité créatrice. *Travail, genre et sociétés,* 3(1), 25–44.

Molinier P. (2006). *Les enjeux psychiques du travail.* Paris, Petite Bibliotheque Payot.

Molinier P. (2020). Le réveil des mauvaises filles. *Multitudes,* 79, 199–204. https://doi. org/10.3917/mult.079.0199

Molinier P., Laugier S., Paperman P. (2009). *Qu'est-ce que le care? Souci des autres, sensibilité, responsabilité.* Paris, Payot.

Moser C., Madeson J. J. (2002). *Bound to Be Free: The SM Experience.* New York, Continuum.

Okin S. M. (1991). Gender, the public and the private. In H. David (Ed.), *Political theory today.* Stanford, CA, Stanford University Press.

Paperman P., Molinier P. (2011). L'éthique du care comme pensée de l'égalité. *Travail, genre et sociétés,* XXVI (2), 189–193.

Pheterson G. (1993). The whore stigma: Female dishonor and male unworthiness. *Social Text,* 37, 39–64.

Poutrain V. (2003). *Sexe et pouvoir: Enquête sur le sadomasochisme.* Paris, Belin.

Rivière J. (1929). Womanliness as a mascarade. *International Journal of Psychanalysis,* X, 303–313, traduit de l'anglais par Victor Smirnoff, La féminité en tant que mascarade, La psychanalyse, vol VII, Paris Puf 1964, réed. in Féminité mascarade. Études psychanalytiques réunies par Marie-Christine Hamon, Seuil, 1994.

Robertiello R. C. (1970). Masochism and the female sexual role. *Journal of Sex Research,* 6(1), 56–58.

Silverman K. (1992). *Male Subjectivity at the Margins.* New York, Routledge.

Tabet P. (2004). *La Grande Arnaque: Sexualité des Femmes et Échanges Économico-Sexuel.* Paris, L'Harmattan.

Vandermeersch, P. (2022). *La chiar de la passion: une histoire de la foi: La flagellation.* Paris, Cerf.

Weiss M. (2011). *Techniques of Pleasure: BDSM and the Circuits of Sexuality.* Durham, NC, Duke University Press.

Williams D. J. et al. (2014). From 'SSC' and 'RACK' to the '4Cs': Introducing a new framework for negotiating BDSM participation. *Electronic Journal of Human Sexuality,* 17, 1–10.

Wiseman J. (1996). *SM 101: A Realistic Introduction.* Emeryville, CA, Greenery Press.

Zelizer V. A. (2005). *The Purchase of Intimacy.* Princeton, NJ and Oxford, Princeton University Press.

RESEARCH METHODS, DESIGN, AND ETHICS

1 The point of taking my subjectivity into account in the interpretation

The objective of my research was to explore the conditions of the practice of female domination in different contexts: in dungeons, in the bedroom, or in public toilets. Although concerned with the organization of the BDSM scene, my interest was mainly directed toward the impact of the capitalist organization of work and gender relations on the interactions between participants. That's why I interviewed people from all over the world, people who are experienced and active in BDSM communities as well as novices who know little about these communities, with little practical experience, spending most of their time in front of their screens alone feeding their fantasy of female domination.

From my position as a researcher, I problematize the place of women in the sexual division of labor and in the economy of gender defense mechanisms and confront the resistance I face as a woman who says something about sexuality. Written in the first person, my research employs a testimonial–type narrative, in which I reveal the encounters that have nourished my work. I have built the research methodology around two stages, field practices and a space to think about this practice in a continuous back and forth. This restitution of the stages of research is necessary because it "relates to the question raised to psychodynamics of work by sociologists of the sexual division of labor: are there collective defenses of the occupation for women?" (Dessors 2012: 27).

Responsible research, above all, requires great restraint so as not to harm the actors and not to compromise working conditions. Thus, I address the difficulty of being in one's place, or better yet, staying in one's place. This is in keeping with the ethics of psychodynamics of work: "never occupy the place of another, never take the role of another, never act on behalf of another" (Dessors 2012: 12).

DOI: 10.4324/9781003258537-2

Aware of the symbolic power of the whore stigma affecting all women as well as the stigma affecting BDSM practices, particular attention was paid to protecting the confidentiality of interviewees. Thus, although practitioners of female domination already use pseudonyms, I refer to them here by their own pseudonyms to further protect their confidentiality except for those who wanted their name to appear explicitly. All of the people I interviewed and quoted in this book know my identity and status as a researcher at the time of the research. A time of restitution-validation with people engaged in practices of female domination was devoted to test my interpretations and with sex workers for Chapters 2 and 4 and to ensure that they do not generate suffering in the working conditions of the people concerned.

I describe in detail in each chapter how and what ethical principles were applied in the different phases of the research and what ethical issues I encountered. In addition, in the chapters discussed, I focus on the values mobilized by practitioners of female domination to evaluate the quality of a session. In doing so, I open the question of professional ethics and of an ethics that is not imposed on the subjects, but that they invent and invest in the very exercise of their practice.

2 Being a woman speaking about sex in the academic sphere

I got to know people involved in the BDSM scene about the same time I started my research on the subject as part of a thesis on female domination (Lugand 2017). I created an account online on social networks like *Le marché aux esclaves* and *FetLife*. I spent a lot of time reading blogs and chatting with dominant women and submissive men online on social networks dedicated to BDSM, and I watched documentaries, movies, and series that are related to those sexual practices, and in particular to female domination. This online focus made sense, because social networks play a key role in facilitating meetups in the world of BDSM. In fact, many adepts of BDSM first discover the scene by answering an online ad, by chatting or interacting on Internet discussion forums, or through DM on platforms like Facebook. From 2012 to 2017, I went to BDSM events, many parties dedicated to female domination, and to numerous munches organized in Paris and Berlin. I also worked for four months with a professional dominatrix in Berlin, whom I assisted in sessions with clients (Chapter 2). In addition, I conducted 30 semi-structured interviews with different practitioners in France and Germany, lasting from one to two hours, with participants aged from 27 to 50 years, from 2011 to 2022.

The first thing to note is that starting a research on the topic of BDSM when I enrolled in January 2013 in Paris was problematic because of its subversive nature – "perhaps too subversive for the university," noted Pascale Molinier, my formal PhD advisor, during my defense. If moments of doubt, indecision, and fear are parts of everyday life and of any project, during this research, these affects sometimes gave way to a real moral panic, on my part and also on the part of my research director Pascale Molinier. Moral panic caused not so much by the fact of speaking about minority sexual practices deemed deviant in an academic setting as by the way I approached them, the way I immersed myself in the field. Let's first note that regardless of the field, the participatory posture of the researchers does not fail to be debated. The danger of immersion research is to break the dialectic of commitment and detachment. The imperative of distancing oneself from the object is particularly thwarted by participation with marginalized and stigmatized groups, caught up in struggles for meaning. In my context, it was difficult to hold my place as a researcher when so abruptly exposed to the whore stigma.

By assuming the approach that I followed in an academic setting, to talk about the work done with professional dominatrixes and about the acts carried out in domination salons and S/M dungeons, I denied the taboo of prostitution and the prohibitions relative to the splitting of the spheres. The choice of the subject itself was debatable. Almost systematically, the question of why I had chosen such a subject came up as well as the question of my personal link with it: BDSM and female domination. Careful attention is paid to the confession of women in the field of sexuality. While one does not systematically ask a person who is doing a thesis on breast cancer, on refugees, etc. how he or she is personally concerned by the subject, the appetite of other researchers to link my desires to my research subject, and/or to discredit the work – personal involvement lacking in concern for objectivity – reveals the workings of gender relations. My work was received with a voyeuristic look. My words were expropriated so that it sticks to a discourse that pre-existed it; my lived experience seized in the only goal to withdraw a satisfaction from it, and I left these interviews extremely tired and diminished, disgusted, and irritated. This is the problem with voyeurism: it prevents listening and understanding because it is an effort to take the word of the other with the sole intention of feeding fantasies. The distance that women must put on the figure of the whore in order to gain and keep the respect of others explains the usual reluctance of female researchers to engage in participant observation in the rough terrain of sexuality.

When I mentioned the difficulties to students in an informal setting, one of them retorted that by choosing to work on this theme, I had to assume the consequences. In other words, I had to pay the price. This makes sense in a form of social organization where women are responsible for the stability of the kinship system. Their sexuality must be controlled, monitored, and limited (Silverman 1984). This explains why, when they reveal their sexuality, female researchers are more likely to highlight the harassment they have experienced in the field, whereas men today are more likely to be able to display their intimate relationships in a given field (Wade 1993). This raises the issue of the asymmetry of respectability of male and female researchers. A woman who puts her desires into discourse gives space in a way that provides new windows of opportunity for discipline and punishment: In the academic sphere through these rituals of confession.

3 Chapter 1: The weight of the social and sexual division of labor

I started to investigate female domination by asking people questions mainly about pleasure, sexual fantasies, fetishes, and desires related to female domination. The fact that I was researching sexuality led me to approach topics of conversation related to sexuality in a common and spontaneous way. I treat sexuality as just another topic in human relationships, and I have tended to overlook the fact that for many people, sexuality is a topic that is only discussed in the private sphere and when one desires an intimate relationship with another. This misunderstanding is linked to a larger context: the separation of the public and private spheres. My fieldwork was thus an opportunity to realize the social weight of this separation, determining the framework of the experiences lived by most of the people I interviewed. I became aware of this as I progressed in my research, by dint of deceptions. I kept repeating the experience and trying to engage in conversation about sexuality as a common topic, but the discrepancy with my male interlocutors kept leading to misunderstandings. For them, engaging in a conversation about sexuality inexorably meant opening up to the practical field. They were incapable of distancing themselves, tirelessly bringing all the subjects back to their preferred practices and desires, and their personal interests: "Me, I'm very visual, Me, I like to touch, Me, I like to lick women's boots." It was therefore not very difficult to remain in a researcher's position, the boredom having the easy tendency to make my desire fade away. In addition, it turns out that – to my surprise – many of these men tried to seduce me by economic means, in this case by paying me gifts or offering me large sums of money: like paying my rent, plane tickets, and very expensive sexy outfits when I had either never met them before or had only met them once or twice. Coming from a modest background and having few financial resources myself, I realized at some point that the pressure of these economic differences would have made me unconsciously feel indebted to these men and bend to their desire. Moreover, at the beginning, the men I met were pushing me toward a dominant female posture that would come close to their "bourgeois" ideal all tight up in Louboutin shoes, which ended any desire to engage in a relationship with them.

This pressure is explained by the fact that in the field, there is a smaller percentage of women and an even smaller percentage of dominant women. Still mystified by the idea of female dominance, I thought that a preponderant place would be given to the expression of women's desire. But these sexual advances, by their form and their contents, tended to shut it down. I quickly became intolerant of this selfishness and began to question the defense that these men frequently mobilized in the face of criticism, namely that as men they had stronger sexual drives than women. It took some time before I transferred this knowledge into my research, before I felt all the imperialism and lack of consideration for women that was behind their use of the term *sexual drive*, as it was understood, in this social (non-Freudian) sense. I realized to what extent men who had not deconstructed this prejudice often imposed their desire. What could be more normal, since they saw their drives in terms of uncontrollable forces? This critical distancing allowed me to take into account the experience of women and the defenses they put in place to fight against these unwanted intrusions. Focusing only on pleasure and gratification ignores the structure of social inequalities in which sexuality takes shape and the social and sexual division of labor. When the latter is taken into account, it becomes clear that "sexuality is simultaneously a realm of restriction, repression and danger as well as a realm of exploration, pleasure and agency in which women live, however." I have attempted to explore in this first chapter – based on semi-structured online and face-to-face interviews – "the tension between sexual danger and sexual pleasure" (Vance 1984).

4 Chapter 2: Investigating as a researcher in salons of domination

For ethical reasons, discussing sexuality in the field remains risky because by revealing their sexual encounters, investigators show that they have used the field for pleasure. Nevertheless, it can be argued that there is a difference between sexuality as a romantic relationship and sexuality as sex or service work. The question then remains whether one can conduct participant observation of sex work. In 2012, I began an immersion as a professional dominatrix, specifically in a domination salon in Berlin for four months. This one is justified by the importance of fee-based services in BDSM communities: professional dominatrixes are present in clubs and promote their services on social networks. Most of the men interviewed, who defined themselves as submissive, resorted to BDSM practices with professional dominatrixes because of their difficulty in meeting dominant women. During parties or in BDSM clubs, there were often professional dominatrixes. For some women, it was a passion and they decided to make it their job. On the website *FetLife* one day, I read an article from a Parisian dominatrix, Maîtresse Céline, who appears in many photos of BDSM parties. She was telling about her being "fed up" with the submissives who criticized the fact that she was charging for her sessions and then accused her of not really dominating for her pleasure. For her defense, she replied that she started to charge for her sessions because most men didn't even have the courtesy to pay for the bottle or bring a little something when they came to her house. Charging was at least a guarantee of an exchange, an assurance that the person would realize the value of the time invested. However, on the side of the men, I meet a very different speech. They all complain in the same way, invoking the lack of naturalness of the sessions: everything would be automatic and devoid of emotion. There was thus an apparent contradiction between the discourse I had been able to gather from the women and that heard from the men as to what a good domination session is which justified my immersion in the salons of domination.

The practice of immersion has been studied and formalized by the sociologist Loïc Wacquant (2007). He defines this form of observation that leads to the routine acquisition of tacit knowledge, and to the understanding of the implicit elements of the respondents' universe as ethnopraxis. Regarding the observation of sexuality, there is a debate among anthropologists (Makowitz and Ashkenazi 1999). Georges Devereux (1980) considers that sexuality cannot be observed by the participatory method. He excludes these experiences so that researchers do not engage with the populations under study in interactions that have a purely instrumental value, which would therefore exclude participant observation with sex workers. Nevertheless, there is a difference between sexuality of which one is the beneficiary, as Devereux speaks about, and sexuality as sex or service work. The question then remains whether it is possible to carry out participant observation of sex work.

I applied to be an assistant for a dominatrix, mentioning I was a student in psychology. It didn't seem to be an issue. That can be explained since many women who charge for their services emphasize the therapeutic aspect of domination sessions. I began my immersion with professional dominatrixes without my supervisor's knowledge. I decided later on to take on this experience and to tell my research director about it. With a touch of apprehension because I was well aware of the taboo character of the practice I was engaged in, I did not know how my director would receive it. She had advised me to publish it under another name, but this posed a problem for me: taking on two identities to avoid being equated with the whore meant admitting my fear of deviating from the "right order of men" by highlighting sexual acts perceived as "illegitimate" and thus accepting the social control exercised over women's sexuality. By refusing to play a double game, I was denying this reality and the dimensions that cause suffering. "The problem is that the denial of perception is a fragile process that remains effective only if it is supported by everyone and everywhere" (Molinier 2000: 36), which isn't the case. In the academic context of my participation in conferences and my research laboratory centered on psychoanalysis and psychodynamic approaches, this work was received softly, as I already mentioned, with suspicion from an academic point of view. In the field, I also had to deal with the suspicion of people involved in the scene who did not believe that one could do these on such a subject and who therefore questioned my legitimacy as a scientist. This affected at first the data collection.

At the same time, I confused the field with my private life during a large part of the investigation, that is to say that I was able, for a certain time, to take my lovers for objects of study and even to become sexually dependent for a moment on the eroticization of the researcher–researched relationship. This loss of control led me to dispossess the people with whom I was involved in affective-sexual relationships and to refuse responsibility for it, unconsciously excusing myself by the fact that these experiences were part of my data collection project. This attitude is not unrelated to the sense of theft I felt in the respondent–investigator relationship. In my case, we can see that the strong involvement not only creates difficulties of an ethical nature but also produces perverse effects in the course of the investigation itself.

Taking on the whore stigma in this context can, however, be considered for the empirical and conceptualized scientific purpose of the social: it allows to avoid "the blinding and dehumanizing effect of scrutinizing people through a prism of prejudice and emotion" (Pheterson 2001). Moreover, this approach allows access to a closed universe other than through interviews, a method that would be "imperfect" because it is also used by agents who control their speech (Jounin and Chauvin 2010). Immersion has the advantage of putting the voice of the people studied back in the foreground by privileging the sharing of experience with them. Furthermore, immersion in domination salons allowed me to get rid of prejudices about the profession of professional dominatrixes and to relativize the points of view of the participants, impregnated by the beliefs and fantasies associated with this profession. Sharing the lives of these sex workers allowed me to have a less distanced, and therefore less abstract, relationship with this profession and to realize its role in the social relations of gender and male domination. This approach allowed me to take into account the defenses I mobilized to face the whore stigma and to question the prejudice according to which paid sexual exchanges would be characterized only by interest and separated from other relationships that would be based on affection. My view of these relationships could not have changed so radically if I had not taken part in the universe of these women and learned, by sharing my time with them, the tacit knowledge of their profession. Eve Berger and pier Vermersch (2006) speak of "bodily epic" to designate certain practices that "engage a break with a certain habitual relationship to the body, to turn towards a type of listening, observation and feeling which opens with the constitution of a specific universe" (Berger and Vermersch 2006: 46). Such an epic allows a renewed listening of the body, a different relation to the body, more present, more subjective, "turned towards something other than what one perceives there in a mechanical relation." The contact with the living bodily interiority can not only participate fully in the description of experience but also, in my case, serve as a foundation for it. This is explained because these bodily experiences take on a strongly significant dimension by the emotional resonances or the spontaneously emerging thoughts that they generate.

5 Chapter 3: My first steps toward demystification and the meeting with gynarchists

My initial questions about female domination were rather naive. I started from an essentialist point of view, and what I wanted to hear and have my interviewees say was that women had "qualities" (such as the ability to listen, to put themselves in the place of the other, and to take care of the other) that predisposed them to dominate better than men. The problem was that this was like saying that these qualities were intrinsic to a female nature. But this did not seem like a problem to me, since I had not taken a course in gender studies at the time. My initial question and subsequent reflections were therefore intertwined with this prejudice about women's supremacy as dominant. One of my first interlocutors on the net – Lèchebottes (see below) – presented a vision of female dominance that has tended not only to confirm my prejudices but also to feed them. His ability to use very poetic and sophisticated language greatly contributed to my own mystification. It helped to make me believe in an enchanted possibility of a different existence in this sense. It represented the first "enchanted" experience.

If this chapter is based, like the others, on semi-directive interviews, in addition, it is built essentially on the narration of our exchanges that took place almost daily over a year. The researcher–researched relationship and its eroticization were particularly problematic with Bootlicker. My encounter with him (see Chapter 3), which saw in my scientific activity the proof of my dominant nature, was decisive in the eroticization of this relationship. As Georges Devereux reminds us, an interview on sexuality, even if it is a scientific interview, is in itself a form of sexual interaction, which can, within certain limits, be entirely lived out and resolved on a purely symbolic or verbal level. Not only Devereux highlights the influence of the erotic relationship on the collection of data, but he also opens "the way to understanding the subjective processes that are at work during the interaction between the researcher and the subject and that affect both protagonists of the interaction in the same way" (Devereux 1980).

In my case, this relationship of seduction is expressed by a loss of control that led me to lose some distance and to let myself be seduced by his epistolary discourse thanks to a power of rhetoric and narcissistic flattery. It is the ethnomethodological trap of the strong implication. The staging of myself and my subjectivity allowed me to highlight the unequal relationship between men and women, to fight against the invisibilization of the mechanisms of power, but there was also a trap in the self-analysis throughout the research: that of spending time talking about oneself and only about oneself, which was all the more facilitated by the compliments that I received, which boosted my narcissism and made me think of myself as being different and better than others and the other women.[1] The investigation became a story of which I became the heroine. The difficulties I experienced highlight "the extreme difficulty of producing a gendered us in the feminine" (Molinier 2006: 241). It allowed me after consideration to become aware of and to take into account the difficulty of getting rid of social gender relations in this research.

6 Chapter 4: Situating my point of view

From 2010 to 2012, between two and four hours a day, I undertook participant observation on social networks in order to build a corpus on female domination in BDSM sexuality, as part of my thesis in social psychology. This participant observation consisted in reading and writing emails, chatting with BDSM practitioners and forum moderators, reading blogs of people identifying themselves as submissive and dominant, and learning about debates on discussion forums. It was completed with additional interviews in 2021. The inclusion of in-depth chat and phone interviews in the methodology allowed for direct questions to be asked of interviewees and for direct discussion of topics relevant to this research. These interviews included money mistresses from different backgrounds and countries, as well as a money slave. Although phone and chat interviews are not equivalent to face-to-face interviews in terms of the ability to read social cues, body language, and facial expressions, the utility of using different interaction systems has been documented by many researchers (Kazmer and Xie 2008). While all women are at risk of being called a whore, a woman is more likely to be called a whore if she sells sex and comes from a working-class background or has a foreign background. As this chapter highlights the voices of some racialized women from working-class backgrounds, great care has been taken to preserve the anonymity of the people mentioned. Screenshots of their walls or blogs have been blurred. All references to personal details have been removed.

The men's online contacts were mostly oriented toward the realization of their sexual fantasy. Indeed, I was inundated, like many other dominant women (see below the ethnography made on the net), with copy and paste messages asking me if I was looking for a submissive, sometimes accompanied by a list of the practices they like and extremely insistent requests. These advances can often be considered harassment. I define sexual harassment, along with anthropologist Jean Gearing, as unwelcome verbal sexual acts and physical advances, remarks, jokes, and obscene gestures that create a hostile social atmosphere for women (Kulick and Willson 1995). I quickly became intolerant of this selfishness, and the frequency of these insistent requests also tended to put me on the reserve during the first contact, and I deactivated my Facebook account for a while. To my great surprise when I reopened my account, the requests were no less insistent, but the questions about the price of my onboard regime services seemed to be real evidence. Also it seems that after the success of *Fifty Shades of Grey*, the BDSM practices have become much more popular among other parts of the population. Obviously the Internet has allowed the introduction of new practitioners who often come from working-class and/or non-white backgrounds. This contrasts with what Margot Weiss says. She points out that at parties, Stammtisch, and workshops, the people interested in BDSM are often white and from the middle and upper classes: access to cultural and economic capital (Weiss 2011). In this respect, Jordi (see Chapter 4), a black submissive man I met on *FetLife*, made me realize how difficult it is for a non-white person to engage in BDSM practices. First, because while growing up he didn't have any contact with white people, outside of teachers, police, church members, and retail workers. Second, because his "family and friends often joked about the weird things white folks did, and twisted sex acts – anal sex, fisting, whipping, birching and golden showers – was one of them."

Yet if experiencing BDSM for a non-white person seemed taboo, the Internet has made it easier for non-white people to engage in BDSM practices. At the early stage of my research, I did not pay attention to these new practitioners and their conception of BDSM because according to the more engaged practitioners on the scene, their practices would not be ethical and therefore could not fit into BDSM practices. At first, I accepted this explanation and did not consider financial slavery as a legitimate object of study. However, this practice started to catch my attention because of the way Taoufik was introduced by the use of Facebook to desire and sexuality. Taoufik, a young man of Moroccan origin whom I met in 2012, was originally interested in foot fetishism and was seeking to know more about his desire and wanted to get involved in the BDSM scene. We met a couple of times in real life and went to a foot fetish party in France in 2014. We then lost contact. I found him again on Facebook three years later and engaged in a conversation with him. He confessed his addiction to the practice of financial slavery which became essential to his sexuality, and even the motor for it. So I began to question him and to be interested in this practice and to seek the voice of these so much decried women. By taking into account their gaze, I had to shift the object of my investigation and thus realize the particularity and subjectivity of my gaze as a white woman from a working-class background on the question posed, which participated in making invisible the voices of a part of the people involved in BDSM practices belonging to a racial minority. One important limitation of this study may be the absence of the voices of young North African women from a lower background. Though I was able to interview in depth two racialized women, they were both graduates and had qualified jobs. The difficulty of contacting more socially vulnerable money mistresses may be explained as a consequence of the attacks made against them, including from some members of the white BDSM community (being a white woman herself), and their young age which may have induced a certain resistance against the researcher. In addition, we could speculate that the tensions inherent to the representation of a transgressive form of femininity (involving both sexual dominance and whore stigma) and, at the same time, the embodiment of a certain misogynist stereotype (the idle woman who profits from men's hardly earned money) might make the *money mistresses* fear moral judgments and being negatively "analyzed" during an interview. Thus, this "politics of silence"[2] can be interpreted as a mode of dealing with those stereotypes.

Notes

1 The representation I had of my work and its scope was in line with the syllogism of the constitution of the female-sexed subject formalized by Kergoat (2001).
2 This expression is borrowed from Evelyn Hammonds, one of the many scholars who has drawn attention to black female sexuality and the way African American women have historically coped with the stereotype. She writes:

> Although some of the strategies used by these black woman reformers might have initially been characterized as resistance to dominant and increasingly hegemonic constructions of their sexuality, by the early twentieth century, they had begun to promote a public silence about sexuality which, it could be argued, continues to the present. This "politics of silence" ... emerged as a political strategy by black woman reformers who hoped by their silence and by the promotion of proper Victorian morality to demonstrate the lie of the image of the sexually immoral black woman.
>
> (Bobo et al. 2004)

Bibliography

Berger E., Vermersch P. (2006). Réduction phénoménologique et épochè corporelle: Psychophénoménologie de la pratique du 'point d'appui'. *Expliciter*, 67, 45–50.

Bobo J., Hudley C., Claudine M. (Eds.) (2004). *The Black Studies Reader*. New York, Routledge.

Dessors D. (2012). *De l'ergonomie à la psychodynamique du travail: Méthodologie de l'action*. Toulouse, Edition érès.

Devereux G. (1980). *De l'angoisse à la méthode dans les sciences du comportement*. Paris, Flammarion.

Jounin N., Chauvin S. (2010). L'observation directe. In S. Paugam (dir.), *L'enquête sociologique*, 143–165. Paris, PUF.

Kazmer M. M., Xie B. (2008). Qualitative interviewing in internet studies: Playing with the media, playing with the method. *Information, Communication & Society*, 11(2), 257–278.

Kergoat D. (2001). Le syllogisme de la constitution du sujet sexué féminin. *Travailler*, 6(2), 105–114, Martin Média.

Kulick D., Willson M. (1995). *Taboo: Sex, Identity and Erotic Subjectivity in Anthropological Fieldwork*. Oxon, Routledge.

Lugand N. (2017). *La domination féminine dans la sexualité BDSM hétérosexuelle*. PhD diss., Université Paris 13 Sorbonne nord.

Makowitz F., Ashkenazi M. (1999). *Sex, Sexuality and the Anthropologist*. Chicago, University of Illinois Press.

Molinier P. (2000). Virilité défensive, masculinité créatrice. *Travail, genre et sociétés*, 3(1), 25–44.

Molinier P. (2006). *Les enjeux psychiques du travail*. Paris, Petite Bibliotheque Payot.

Pheterson G. (2001). *Le prisme de la prostitution*. Paris, l'Harmattan, Bibliothèque du féminisme.

Silverman K. (1984). Histoire d'O: The construction of a female subject. In S. Vance (Ed.), *Pleasure and Danger: Exploring Female Sexuality*. London, Routledge and Kegan Paul.

Vance S. (1984). *Pleasure and Danger: Exploring Female Sexuality*. London, Routledge and Kegan Paul.

Wacquant L. (2007). Parias urbains. Ghetto, banlieues, État. Une sociologie comparée de la marginalité sociale, La Découverte, coll. "La Découverte/Poche."

Wade P. (1993). Sexuality and masculinity in fieldwork among Colombian blacks. In D. Bell, P. Caplan, W. J. Karim (Eds.), *Gendered Fields: Women, Men and Ethnography*, 199–214. London and New York, Routledge.

Weiss M. (2011). *Techniques of Pleasure: BDSM and the Circuits of Sexuality*. Durham, Duke University Press.

1

PLEASURE IN FEMALE DOMINATION PRACTICES AND FEMALE LABOR

1.1 Introduction

Like many people interested in BDSM sexuality and female domination, I began my journey by reading blogs, books, and a lot of documentaries and films about these sexualities. Pornographic or erotic films depicting BDSM sexualities began to gain visibility in the 1980s. According to Denis Altman, a sociologist and political scientist, the campaign to introduce condoms into sexual life, due to the proliferation of AIDS, has induced an awareness and produced changes in sexual practices, developing a new interest in non-penetrative sexuality in the Western world (Altman 2001).

Films about female domination like the French film *Maîtresse* by Barbet Schroeder (1975), just like the film *My Mistress* directed by Stephen Lance (2014), attempt to portray female domination and dominatrixes well by emphasizing the therapeutic aspect of female domination. Other films such as *Die Flambierte Frau* (Ackeren 1983) give space to the dimensions of care, in particular by emphasizing the psychological and ethical dimensions of this profession. The recognition of these dimensions would give credit to these women in their capacity to help, look after, and guide the other toward a more fulfilling life. Thus, behind every sexually dominant, hard, indifferent woman, there would be a hidden caring, empathetic, and emotional woman who would make the other a "good dominatrix."

Classically, in these movies and in other places, it is acknowledged that the degree of success in a session of domination varies according to the personality of the dominatrix and that of the submissive (Varrin 2004). Without denying the role of the individual variations during a successful session of domination, it is necessary to introduce another level of analysis and to emphasize the division of labor between men and women, where women in general have fewer privileges than men and men can pay for sexual services for which they are prescribers,

DOI: 10.4324/9781003258537-3

recipients, and evaluators. Let's note in this line that all the films mentioned on female domination deal with venal domination, i.e. as a service to the male gender. The division of labor is expressed by certain men who buy sexual services of dominatrixes, and therefore is also represented in their fetishism like the fetishism of the feet, the stilettos, or the leather boot by means of the commercialization of its sexuality.

But the commercialization of sexuality is not the only thing that impacts practitioners of female domination. When interactions between men and women are governed by a division of labor that tends to place men in a situation of domination over women, the latter's material interest often motivates them to place themselves in the service of the man. I have observed that the sexual practices, either performed in casual encounters or in lasting bonds, all rely on the care work that maintains the link between submissive men and dominant women in BDSM communities. Knowledge and skills developed at work operate in a non-professional context. Moreover, the exploitation faced by women in the domestic sphere and their lack of time for fantasy life are reflected in their BDSM practices. On the other side, in our economic context, "the most successful are those who seem not to understand the degree to which their success and their capacity for action depend on who is serving them" (Laugier 2010: 116). Their conception of care in sexuality may conflict with those of women who have the constraint of performing these tasks in their work. Sexual practices and work are then interconnected. It leads me to criticize and overcome another dichotomy, "on which the theories of care have remained more discreet until now: the sexuality/work dichotomy" (Molinier et al. 2009: 233).

This chapter focuses on the interviews of participants who practice female domination in a non-commercial way. I show how the colonization of the economy on the private ground shifts us from the expanding service economy to the fissures of what appears to be the most private and therefore the most hidden. It complicates the space-time continuum for people who practice female domination in a non-commercial way and updates the psychological permeability between professional and personal times shown by researchers in ergonomics.

1.2 Definition of care work

The intersection of the cultural history of care and its provider with the role of care in BDSM reveals the dependent relationship of BDSM ethics to the philosophy/history of care work. For Joan Tronto, an ethic of care is a personal, social, moral, and political approach to life that assumes that all human beings need, receive, and give care to others (Tronto 1993). Care is based on experiences or activities that consist in providing a concrete response to the needs of others – domestic work, care, education, support, or assistance. Then, it encompasses a range of activities drawing a line between tending people, their home, and their bodies. In this respect, there exists a continuum of sexual service and care work, from sex work to nursing, housekeeping, helping, and educating.

Care is "transmitted" through work – work in the broad sense. Care work cannot be reduced to the sole form of salaried work. Care work is also situated in other types of relationships such as friendship, solidarity, or filiation. This work is done mainly by women, but it is not inherent to the psycho-cognitive development of women. Care is indeed separated from femininity. The care perspective breaks with the naturalistic conception of the different tasks between men and women. This goes in line with the researches in psychodynamics of work that have shown that work experience transforms the individual, and therefore, these experiences are to be taken into account to think about psychological processes generally attributing to someone's personality or sexual identity. Thinking of care as a job allows us to separate it theoretically from femininity and love (Molinier et al. 2009: 15).

This being said, the constraint of care work is mainly exerted on women. It is, of course, expressed in the form of the labor market. In fact, these are the jobs occupied in a priority way by poorly qualified women from working-class backgrounds and economically displaced migrants. But the execution of care work is also related to identity injunctions. Although the independence of action and judgment is considered one of the characteristics of adulthood, it is above all in function of the care and the well-being that a woman provides to others that she judges herself and is judged (Gilligan 1982). Studies confirm, like the study on stepfamilies in England by McCarthy, Edwards, and Gillies, that there are strong differences in the construction of kinship between women and men: the ethic of child care is primary among mothers. The ever-present responsibility of women for children and the lesser responsibility of men turn into demands for psychological and material work (McCarthy et al. 2003). We are not yet released from this model, and the scenarios that give shape to the conflicts of the dominant women in the BDSM scene of today draw the contours of their sexual fantasies by placing them in an alternative position that opposes gender norms in the long run. In our context, it is difficult to be a mother while being a sexually dominant woman. It is not easy, and sometimes the social pressure pushes women to stop dominating men for a long time, among other things, because they have been made to understand that if they are too dominant, "they will never find a man," as Clara told me.

Broadly speaking, care work reflects the relations of inequality in society; not only is the provision of care unequal, with some receiving more care than others, but also those who provide care tend to have fewer resources than those who receive it. Most care workers are women, and consequently, care work is usually considered to be a non-market activity or of low economic value as well as low social value due to the presence of dirt, closeness with the bodies, and intimacy (Boris and Parrenas 2010). It is those care activities confined to the subaltern category that focus attention, contributing to the marginalization and undermining of the importance of care.

To redefine care is to denounce a process of marginalization of its activities (Molinier et al. 2009). Tronto proposes to address this problem by claiming a political dimension of care. More fundamentally, she advocates rethinking the relationship between morality and politics. The care perspective emphasizes the *interdependence and vulnerability* of all; no one can claim self-sufficiency, and it demands that we stop propagating the myth of autonomy and the self-made man. In reality, each of us is engaged in a complex network of care relationships. To question the boundaries of morality is therefore to question the moral value of liberal individualism and to propose the elaboration of a new political ethic. From then on, Joan Tronto engages in a reflection on good care. She identifies four necessary phases. The first, defined as *caring about*, consists of first noticing that a need exists and that a related service is required. The second, *taking care of*, refers to taking charge, assuming a responsibility. In the third, *caregiving*, effective care work and its competence are put in evidence (Tronto 1993: 158). The fourth element is the patient's/family's *responsiveness* to care (Tronto, 1993). It is important to ensure that the patient's care needs are met. Finally, good care is based on four elements of a care ethic, namely (a) *attention*, (b) *responsibility*, (c) *competence*, and (d) *resonance*.

1.3 Care in the definition of female domination

We cannot question BDSM relationships today without taking into account the turn of the 1980s–1990s and the emphasis on interdependence, trust, and care in BDSM relationships.

The particularity of female domination is the emphasis on the quality of care. In fact, in the heterosexual BDSM literature where women are dominant, there is more emphasis on the lust of submissive men than on the lust of dominant women. This is related to the fact that much of this literature is about professional female domination and is written by professional female dominatrixes. Though each mistress has her own style of dominance and D/S preference, "her business success depends on her customer satisfaction. She must therefore maintain a fine balance between giving the submissive what he wants, showing that she is still in charge, and satisfying her own dominant persona" (Graham Scott 1997: 211). Maîtresse Françoise, a French dominatrix, in her book of the same name, explains how she holds herself back from having an orgasm during a session with a submissive, and while "she cannot hold back from having an orgasm, she succeeds under a mask of Hercule to remain unperturbed, inviolable" (Foucault 1994: 58): the dominatrix must keep control.

The notion of the gift of domination for the submissive is underlined by Claudia Varrin, a professional dominatrix, an active member of fetish scenes (especially in New York), and the author of *Female Dominance: Rituals and Practices* (Varrin 2004). If the acceptance of pain on the part of bottoms can be seen as a gift from one partner to another, according to Claudia Varrin, "the gift of dominance includes the accepting of the **responsibility** and although the responsibility is temporary, the acceptance makes the gift of dominance as rare and special as that of submission and neither one should be undervalued" (Varrin 2004: 20).

One part of the "domina's gift to her submissive would be her *ability to listen* to [(*attention*)] and accept her submissive's sexual desires as well as the dominatrix's willingness to step behind the veil and the wish to enact his fantasies with him" (*caregiving*). If there is a remark on the desire of women, it is after that of the submissive. Other facets of the dominant gifts are her creativity and imagination, and the time and energy she puts into the fantasy enactment. "It is reckoned that imagination, sensitivity, intelligence and eloquence were the attributes of a successful mistress" (*competence*). Domination means work for the domina,

> unlike the submissive, for whom the playtime is all fun and games dominant women must keep bottoms in a constant and increasing state of sexual tension, and must also be able to understand the needs and limits of the submissive party, to satisfy her needs and test her limits.
>
> *(Varrin 2004: 20)*

What prevails is the idea of practical intelligence. Knowing "how to bring the submissive to the surface" (Hart 2003) means emphasizing practical effectiveness, evaluating a "good session" based on practice. The exercise of this form of intelligence would be linked to the ability to give mentioned by Varrin in *Female Dominance: Rituals and Practices*, as it is inseparable from the care given to the bottoms.

The role this form of intelligence plays and the ability of the submissive to respond to the desires of his mistress, to establish an emotional connection, to be sensitive, and to have a sincere desire to please are important too (*responsiveness*). This means that the dominatrix doesn't want a robot toy but someone who has "common sense and intelligence, and a desire to please." In a perfect world, as Varrin mentioned, when she needs a cigarette, the submissive would light it for her.

Therapeutic aspect of the practices sometimes considered in terms of a healing process or sadotherapy, and the educational dimension for the submissive "teaching him the manners his upbringing should have instilled in him" (Varrin 2004: 22) are parts of the main criteria for evaluating a good session. Some dominatrix women consider female domination as a catharsis for important men.

> The dominance and assertiveness of the woman enables the man relief from his usual social role of having to make decisions. She relieves him of [*responsibility*]. He is free to lose himself in this other world, in submission to a powerful woman.
>
> *(Weinberg and Kamel 1983: 82)*

This notion of the submission as an abandonment of control and responsibility is also put forward by other dominatrixes. Maîtresse Françoise states that punishing for the faults that they think they have committed or the faults that they think they will commit in the future turns them "into dead men so that 'they are re-born in her power." She listens to their emotions and calms their pain: "the ones

I just caused and the one of their life" (Foucault 1994: 55). For Varrin, being the submissive also gives a safe haven to release pent-up frustrations and/or get rid of fear and anger, not carry them along.

Dominatrixes base their BDSM practices on ethical values and adopt practices that are safe, sane, and consensual, such as RACK, PRICK, or 4Cs. They seek to inform and make their client aware of risk and consider health and safety in their play (O'Nomis 2013: 2373). Varrin insists that she wants subs to trust her enough to reveal their *vulnerabilities* to her: she expects them to be as honest as possible about any medical condition he may have as she needs to know the physical limitations to mitigate risk as much as possible (Varrin 2004). Another dimension that must be mentioned in this respect is the importance of hygiene. Working as a dominatrix involves doing the legworks of cleaning and sterilizing instruments such as cane jars, framed surgical instruments, and studded leather hoods (O'Nomis 2013).

From this perspective, dominant women can be described with the same vocabulary as for nurses. In Claudia Varrin's world, dominatrixes are far from "the well-known role of the cruel and authoritarian woman" (De M'Uzan 1951: 137).

For these authors, BDSM practices are considered as a learning space, a transitional space, of transformation of the submissive. The role of the dominatrix is to allow the bottom to accompany, to reassure, to understand, and in other words, to heal.

The curative dimension of masochism is reinforced by other mediations, in particular by symbolic representations. Bob Flanagan's artistic work, especially *Visiting Hours*, first shown at the Santa Monica Museum of Art in 1992, is particularly interesting in highlighting the convergence between disease and S/M. Bob Flanagan was born in 1952 in New York with a degenerative disease called mucoviscidosis. The disease, which causes breathing difficulties, pneumonia, and infections, forced him to spend much of his childhood in the hospital. Prisoner of his body that makes him suffer, subjected to the disease, and dependent on the medical profession, Bob Flanagan built his identity through S/M practices. His engagement in sadomasochistic practices would have allowed him to live longer by sublimating his malaise instead of passively enduring the suffering. This is in any case what he suggests in the documentary on his life and work: *Sick: The Life and Death of Bob Flanagan: Supermasochist* (1996).

1.4 The nature of care practice among the interviewees

Thinking about the psychological processes generally attributed to sexual identity, my approach in the psychodynamics of work reverses the perspective of the subject that precedes work. Women initiate practices of female domination with dispositions developed by the labor of care; it is then in this way that many dominatrixes construct their sexual identity. As Mistress Jamiali says:

> I think that female care takes on maternal notes in domination, because our model of someone who is dominant over our lives while caring is first our

mothers. As a woman who has had children, yes, a lot of my current domination mirrors how I mothered them. I think for women caregiving inevitably is going to slide into anticipatory care, and then what I would call
prescriptive care. For example, I give care to my submissives by saying
"You can't eat a cookie after a full meal, because you worked hard today
and eating cookies is not going to make you feel good." It's all about caring
for someone and wanting them to feel better in the long run, but it's inevitably attached to boundary building.

I do think that a lot of men find that sort of caregiving activates any
unresolved mother issues. Some will respond to it angrily. "You're not my
mother, don't pull that shit!" Some are more at peace with that energy,
and will laugh and say "Yeah, mom ... you're right, what are we doing for
dinner?" Both my submissives respond not from an adult place but from
a child place and say, "Yes, Mommy. I'm a good boy/girl and I will wait
to have the cookies till after dinner." That's not always what comes out of
their mouth, but that's where their head is. I know both of them had ne-
glectful and abusive childhoods and they genuinely need more mothering
to "finish growing up" on some level. For some women that would be off
putting. For me, it's what I like. It simplifies my life for me to be in charge
of theirs. They need some mothering. I want to give it. There is no real
kinky play in the mom/son or mom/daughter sense. But that energy is
there 24 hours a day, in our house and among all of us.

If care is sometimes confused with a way to express love in the accounts of some
interviewees and has a certain feminine nature, it exceeds the limits of the private business and begins to think of itself as what it is, that is to say a job. Then,
the narrative changes, bringing out ambiguous dimensions of emotional life and
other levels of *responsibility*. We see in a comment left by Mistress Jamiali in a discussion group on care "how care's responsibilities are fragmented along gender
lines" (Molinier et al. 2009):

I care to take both the submissive and slave that I own. They both have
severe mental illnesses, and having an orderly environment, healthy food,
and someone to make sure they take their meds makes the difference between them being able to be contributing members of the workforce or,
well, not. They value my work and the time and effort it takes greatly. In
return, they take care of me financially. They help me overcome years of
abuse from a former partner by encouraging me. They love me and support
me in infinite ways on a daily basis. And, of course, they give me their submission and let me control so much of their lives, to our mutual pleasure
and benefit. They both had less than ideal childhoods in several respects.
In some ways, I am "remothering" them. They are learning that they are
loved and wanted. They are learning how to cope with frustration and anger. They are purging old mental tapes and learning how to coexist in the
flow of having a chronic illness, so one can have a life around it.

The care perspective here emphasizes the dependence and vulnerability of all, including those who are considered the most important, those who have succeeded professionally and personally. The interview highlights that the support given in domestic tasks is to be considered to better understand the success of some having more available brain time to devote to their work and projects.

Care dimensions appear in the expected personality traits of a dominatrix, but a whole bunch of fetishes such as medical fetish, lactophilia, and baby bottle fetish refer to the practices of care, as in the case of Simon, a 46-year-old German diaper fetishist:

> My interest in wearing diapers goes way back to my youth. I wore my first diaper again at the age of 16. Then, I really started a diaper "career," i.e. a steadily increasing process. Occasional diaper wearing became every weekend, then every night, then out of the house, finally 24/7 (even at work). I've gotten into a bit of a routine in the realm of diaper wearing. Morning and evening diaper changes (I get by with two a day thanks to fairly thick diapers) are just part of the routine – like showering and brushing teeth. I have accessories (rubber pants, nursing bodysuits) that I can rely on. Why diapers? I just like everything about it. The feeling when wearing them. The feeling of wetting. The smell of the warm, wet diaper and rubber pants. The convenience of wearing diapers (no more trips to the bathroom).

In addition, many sexual practices and fantasies of female domination refer to the care work provided by women such as nurse and teacher games, babysitting services. There are many ads and groups that have these roleplays as their subject on *FetLife*.

> I have been involved in [*adult/child roleplay*] for over 10 years. This is not punishment centered, or sexual, more as a service for those who need to be treated as a baby. I do bottle feedings, hold, play with babies and toddlers. I change both wet and messy diapers. I can also be a playmate or baby for you to care for, the breastfeeding, Mommy … etc.

While her practices have the advantage of emphasizing authority in connection with her little-recognized caregiving profession, it is only by reflecting on these practices after the fact that the political value of care can be recognized.

This can be complicated by the fact that the recognition of what we owe to the care of others is deficient. Those activities remain invisible simply because "they have no objective expression, and do not produce an object. This work not only has no material expression, but its effectiveness depends in part on its very invisibility" (Molinier 2006: 145). Paying attention to the needs of others erases its own traces, disappearing as an effort at work. In the following section, we will see how this interferes with the practices of female domination.

1.5 What limits the notion of service among men?

According to Joan Tronto, the people who seem to be the most autonomous are in fact those who benefit the most from the care of others (Tronto 1993). It seems that people who are mostly beneficiaries of care, used to *the privilege of being served* without having to think about it, would find it harder to integrate the notion of service. Emily notes that her boyfriend wanted to serve her wine, but when she wanted water, sometimes he did and sometimes he didn't because it didn't fit his service fantasy. In fact, the representation that the submissives make of the service would serve above all to feed their own fantasies and fetishes.

Yet for many dominatrixes, a person who does not want to serve could not claim to be submissive. This does not prevent many dominatrixes to fall prey to submissives who are, in fact, serving their own fantasy. This is the kind of relationship that Sonia experienced.

> We soon became involved in BDSM where the mistress is in a very S/M position, that is to say, beatings, bondage, blindfolded. A lot of practices which allowed in fact to satisfy his fantasies. At the time, I was working on the management of the State debt in Paris. It was 2012, in the middle of the economic crisis. So I came home exhausted from my day, exhausted with stress, and I wasn't always open to start sessions. He really had this need. The notion of service for him was always sexual. At least sexualized. Even to do the dishes, I had to feminize him, to put a dildo in his ass. That was it. He didn't do it on his own. He didn't have any notion of service on that side. He would only do a service if the service was sexualized. In this case there was no problem ... On the other hand, if I said to him "go wash the dishes" while being [dressed] in jeans and a T-shirt, it became a real burden for him and he made it felt. So he spent his days on the Internet, on BDSM forums getting excited, reading a lot of stories on a lot of sites that also made him have fantasies. I had my day's work ahead of me, and when I got home I had to cook and take care of the kid.

To say that desires, such as the desire for the submissive to serve a woman by doing the housework, are implanted in our social and political imaginary, and to seek to understand how these desires can affect our involvement in society must not leave aside the fact that the modalities of desires are the effect of the mechanisms by which society is organized. This dialog sample shows how Sonia's partner can feed his fantasies all day long, having all the space to care about him, while Sonia works full-time, taking care of her son and the kitchen, which creates the conditions for a patriarchy disguised under the guise of BDSM. The relationship of domination appears to be very unequal to Sonia's disadvantage. Here it is well the problem of the division of work of the tasks that is questioned about. The domestic work testifies of different cuttings when men have the load of it. When it is done by women, it is free and treated as a family obligation, but when it is done by men, it is treated *as a political contribution to society that requires retribution (monetary or benefit in kind)*. Women traditionally assigned to the domestic sphere have been able to develop knowledge and awareness of the world they receive through caregiving. On the contrary, for men, domestic tasks are considered as a service put at their disposal or as a fantasy of submission.

On the side of submissive men, serving a woman means occupying a position that is inverted in relation to virility, the key psychological factor of which is the shame of being considered a woman (Molinier 2000). By virility, we must understand a defense collectively constructed by men in the spaces of male sociability (in particular at work) to fight against fear and *vulnerability*, which allows them to establish their privileges on self-control. Proving that one is "manly" by denying one's *vulnerability* allows one to be part of the dominant group. In the case of submissives, as Patricia, a 49-year-old living in the US, states, the shame and status of abjection associated with being treated as a woman is erotic:

> Both of us are major spankos so that alone doesn't really take him down a few pegs. But when I call him on his attitude or mini-road rage and paddle him on the spot – including at parks or outside off the road – it does take him down a few pegs. When I take him up the butt (something he doesn't like but does for me within the context of our relationship), I often do a role reversal, telling him how he's only receiving what so many wives receive and saying all the time how I want him to be my submissive wife and take it up the butt whenever I want. I even sometimes combined small penis humiliation with my pegging enjoyment (saying how he is fortunate that he has such a cute, fuckable bottom since his penis is so small).

The humiliating character is clearly denoted in some representations of the service fantasy.

However, the sexual practice of service is also about work. And as Pierre-Tigre, a French sub of 25 years old, writes so well, work introduces effort and boredom:

> I never realized before the mindfuck effect that can come from housekeeping. You fantasize about the session for days: You imagine yourself in the apartment with a broom in your hand. You lend this trivial image an intense power of satisfaction. What's that draft between the two? A perfect example of magical thinking. To take one thing and replace it in thought with another more perfect one as a source of enjoyment, "this is the mechanics" of fetishism in full swing. Now you arrive at the apartment, trembling with impatience. Let's suppose that your partner, gone for a tricycle ride, has left you the keys: you are alone, and you find yourself in front of this damn broom. There's this incredible moment when all the feverish excitement you had wrapped up in it just collapses under the disappointment. Suddenly, domestic tasks appear for what they are: tedious, boring, repulsive enough that someone might conceive the wish to let

someone else do it for them. So why does it have to be you, and what do you get out of it? So what was it about it that excited you? For a moment, you find yourself absolutely stranger to your desire and what you are doing is no longer magical.

Thus, the practice of the service to the dominant women confronts certain men subjected to their fantasy of

> enchanted care, the one from which benefits the beauty and the beast in the film of Cocteau or the body of the servants is reduced to the poetic expression of their utility, candelabra arms, hand pours carafe, a care without face and which does not ask anything in return, melted in element esthetic of the decor.
>
> *(Molinier et al. 2009)*

The beautiful text of Pierre-Tigre shows that the work of psychic elaboration that the subversion of the defensive virility implies is long, challenging, and tricky. The number of texts published since embarking on this subject on his *FetLife* profile testifies that this work is never finished.

What can then enable men such as John to have another point of view? How did he acquire the skills of care to best serve dominant women?

> First, his father was laid off right after he was born, the third of three children. This evidently was a shocker for his parents because his father did not have a high school diploma and his mom had quit her job when the two got engaged prior to their marriage (what different times those were, huh?). His mom found a job and continued to work until retirement. John's father stayed home and was an early version of "Mr. Mom" until John went to school. He thinks this had a major worldview he still holds today. He saw his father cooking and doing laundry (the one thing I always do, ironically), cleaning up and vacuuming. He said that his father and mom had an incredibly loving relationship and remembers seeing his dad always rubbing lotion on his mom's feet and scratching them for her pleasure. It was a normal thing. Second, John is a feminist. He raised three confident daughters who expect equal treatment. I do think that serving me fits fine in that world setting and his upbringing. Finally, John speaks about his privilege – having a degree at 21 years old, being accomplished with his career, and being a white male over 6 foot tall.

As this interview sample shows, the fact that children are working and that their work can influence their development is related to moral psychology. The ethical question of the distribution of power is indeed a matter of perception and attention, as Martha Nussbaum already stated. Moral competence is not only a matter of knowledge or affection, but it is also a matter of learning how to express oneself adequately and of educating oneself to sensitivity (Nussbaum 2006).

1.6 The dominant women crumbled under the weight of the quantity of submissive men

1.6.1 The desire of women in question

On dating BDSM sites like *FetLife*, the participation of men is greater than women.[1] Not only would men outnumber women, but among women the percentage of dominants would be relatively low. According to the interviewees, the supply of submissives is always greater than the demand of the mistresses, which tends to reinforce the power of women in their choice of partners. As I read in Gala Fur's book *Dare to Know Everything about SM*: "Only the dominatrix can be disdainful and pompous. The most unbearable mistress will always have her fan club!" (Fur 2004). Jasmin's interview confirms what the men I interviewed said in my field survey on the net about the lack of dominant women.

> There is a difference between the amount of submissive men and the few women and it's like a market. Theoretically there's a lot of choice but the dynamics are really weird, there's an incredible number of submissive men applying to few dominant women, and that means there's incredible competition, and at the same time whenever submissive men meet dominant women they're very invasive, because they're afraid it's going to be the only time it happens, and they're doing everything they can to make it happen because they haven't been able to live with it for so long. I know a lot of submissive men who haven't done anything for years and they are desperate and I understand that when you can't live your sexuality. The problem is that I am not the salvation army, I can't take every submissive man under my wing.

Because of the scarcity of mistresses, some submissives even come to lose hope of meeting a real dominatrix. In a discussion on Facebook, "doormat slave," who has been a submissive for ten years, says he has never met a "dominatrix woman who doesn't do this for money." He is convinced that dominatrix women who do this for their pleasure do not exist! Relatedly, I remember vividly the number of times I had to listen to submissives complaining that they could not find dominant women, and that all women they have met until now lacked genuine concern for female dominants and instead had self-serving motives, mostly financial. This idea is a leitmotif easy to find in many books about sadomasochism. This lack of involvement is generally explained by the sexist idea that *women have less sexual drive* and therefore think less about sex than men (Scott 2014: 28). However, when women feel comfortable enough to express their desire for domination, as in Christine's case, it is remarkable enough:

> Power and control are erotic but also go past eroticism to a place where they soothe and bolster my psyche. Causing pain is straight up erotic, even more so when mixed with control. Watching people react to what I do is

erotic to me. I also have a very strong deviance kink, so if I am getting off doing something that is a serious departure from normal sexuality, that works more for me. (Aka, an orgasm for me because I'm teasing him and not letting him come, but letting him feel me come on his cock, is bigger for me than just a straight up woman on top orgasm.) So being the woman in charge is deviant, hurting people for fun is deviant, ruining his orgasm is deviant, hurts him, makes him react to me … all sorts of good things in one package!

Other women have approached head-on the erotic pleasure taken in the female domination. Jasmin was quick to describe to me her fetishes "which are pain, blood, very masculine things, bondage as an active person because [she] doesn't [let herself] get tied up."

That being said to my question, "What were/are your initial fantasies related to female domination?" most of the women I interviewed did not answer, glossed over it like Franzi, or skirted around the question with the help of scientific discourses to explain their orientation toward female domination. According to them, there is a continuity between personality and passive or active sexual orientation. The strength of character, the spirit of initiative, and the spirit of rebellion already present in childhood are invoked to explain "naturally" their sexual orientations. My research confirms that often what is not said, or what we don't speak about, is not thought of all the less when the disposition is taken, and that it becomes a mode of being in the world, as part of one's nature. Sonia and many women practicing female domination think that taking charge and running everything is part of their *nature* and a certain *dominant nature*.

Nature is used here as a moral justification for socially deviant behaviors that would be irrepressible: "Before I got into BDSM, in my sexuality it was always me who was in charge of everything." It comes back as a leitmotif to the answer of the question about the origin of fantasies as with Aline. This naturalness attached to the role taken in BDSM relationships gives her a certain feeling of confidence:

I had Maxime and I realized that yes I like to lead, I have this need. But in my daily life too, at work too. How many times my friends told me, but you are really bossy. You are in charge, you decide everything. When we organize our weekends with our friends, every time it's me who takes the organization of the thing. I have always decided my life and, as far as I was allowed to do so, the lives of those who were close to me. But it's not something I'm looking for. It's an [*instinctive*] thing with me. It is natural. This authority somewhere is [*natural*].

Knowing the risks incurred by women who speak about sexuality, I interpret their attitude as a defense to protect themselves from the risk linked to the whore stigma. This risk is all the more present when this sexuality departs from the "good," "normal," and "natural" sexuality, which should ideally be heterosexual, conjugal, monogamous, non-commercial, and vanilla (Rubin 2001). It consists in reversing the relationship to the constraints inherent in the sexual division of labor by making it look like a freely consented choice, which is similar to muliebrity. If muliebrity is, like virility, a defensive construction, it is not, however, its symmetrical counterpart. If virility can serve as a borrowed identity in that it promises valorization and success with women, muliebrity refers only to the depreciation and erasure of the self (Molinier 2000). Indeed, this defense is built on prejudices that reinforce the invisibilization of women's work. In fact, by putting forward the dimensions of care to define themselves as dominant, they make the constraint attached to these activities disappear. They thus reinforce the prejudice that women are naturally more caring than men and that it is therefore natural for them to take on more care tasks than men. In other words, they update the assumption that the care activities these women perform to meet the needs of others are based on a psychological predisposition, which is part of their nature, and not on a series of experiences or activities.

1.6.2 The all-powerful male sexual drive in question

The relationship lived under the fear of shortage prevents the person from paying attention to the space of the dominant women. According to Maria, a 55-year-old French dominatrix, many men note the difficulty of making meetings on the Internet and wonder: are there only professional dominatrixes? Or why don't women ever respond to the ads we post or the messages we send them? Their impersonal messages focused on their sexual interest would be at issue. Many women explicitly write on their profile that they are tired of receiving access messages about their desires and consider it rude. How can we explain that these men who want to live their sexuality are not listening? The prejudice that men would have stronger sexual drives than women would be in question.

This prejudice of lesser sexual drive in women often leads submissive participants to use the service of professional dominatrixes (Graham Scott 1997) and would thus get used to consider the practices of female domination as a service. Many dominatrixes are paying the price and are fed up with "pseudo-submissive" profiles that simply list their wants and needs (I have been a target) and mention that these wish lists stifle their desire, that they are not being paid to fulfill the fantasies of submissive men and that this attitude prevents them from creating a long-term relationship with authenticity and emotional intensity. For Jasmin, the attitude of submissives is explained by their education.

> Me: Do you feel like a lot of times they think you're a domina pro?
> Jasmin: Yeah, unconsciously. I tell them, Hey, you think I'm a prostitute, and *they're shocked because they're not aware because they don't perceive it*. It's a combination of total desperation and habit too. They are used to getting things from a woman. I am at home, my dinner is waiting for me, and

many men are frightened when they see that I don't offer service. In their environment, their mother served them, cooked for them, washed their clothes, and in fact it is a habit they grew up with. And for a lot of heterosexual men sex is a service, it doesn't matter if you're a pro dom [venal dominatrix] or a normal prostitute, or in a striptease or a movie, you get a naked woman serving. It's a service they get without realizing it. They are looking forward to deal with a dominant woman and to getting great service.

Women's desires are denied, and men prefer to avoid thinking about it. I argue that it is because it carries the risk of leading them to wonder to what extent they themselves might be susceptible to exercising a form of violence against women and disadvantaged people, possibly *without perceiving* it, if only by endorsing it through their "*indifference of the privileged person*" (Molinier 2000). They may think that they had to *invisibilize* those differences to be in a relationship with a woman they are submissive to. Ironically, in their opinion, it is the woman who is taking advantage of them. The ones who were on the side of violence were women who took advantage of them. Many submissives complain that they can't find women who are genuinely interested in BDSM, but they find women who want it only for their money, in other words, prostitutes. Their projection of violence, aggression, onto women through the figure of the whore could be understood as a way of refusing the empathic encounter, a defense to protect them from the suffering generated by "the risky listening" of their subjective experience.

1.7 On the (in)awareness of vulnerability according to gender

Paying attention to a dominant woman means also paying attention to her space, attention to the relational modalities, and attention to her fragilities – without excluding, of course, the questions of asymmetry. Failing to insert *vulnerability* into the contract between the dominatrix and the submissive prevents attention to the other's need for space that allows her to breathe and resilience.

Even if better economic opportunities can obviously keep women away from the bonds of marriage, as in the case of Sonia who "earns a good living and has a good salary," we can only observe the opposite situation: women are much less hesitant and ambivalent about commitment and stable long-term relationships. Autonomy is, of course, not foreign to women; it is even at the heart of their project of emancipation. But when transposed to the private sphere, the ideal of *autonomy* interferes with the demand for recognition in love relationships and operates within a fundamentally unequal distribution structure of autonomy. According to E. Illouz, not only do men need less recognition from women than the other way around, but both men and women need recognition from men (Illouz 2012). Indeed, "the masculine identity was born from the renunciation of the feminine" (Kimmel 2005: 32). In this perspective, the male gender identity is shaped against the female identity and the need for dependence and sharing, which makes men less able to create or desire a long-term bond. According to Anne Vincent Buffault, in the middle of the 19th century, commitment became an essentially feminine prerogative; men did not recognize this need and the condition of *vulnerability* that falls to us all (Buffault 1991). This sample from Sonia's interview is particularly illuminating in comprehending the interactive dimension of *vulnerability* and *domination*. The unequal relationship between Sonia and her lover works because both people are aware of the situation. Sonia's lover is aware of the control he has over Sonia, and Sonia finds it difficult to ignore it, being threatened with abandonment if she refuses to fulfill his desires. They passed a contract orally before beginning their relationship where he said he wanted to commit himself and "to be a father for her son." This contract did not have consequences since the lover of Sonia will end up leaving without worrying about this child and about the way in which she can manage this transition. The reason for this is that, as Goodin notes, our moral obligations do not rely on a contract but draw their "moral and binding power" *from the awareness of each person's vulnerability in the relationship* (Goodin 1985). Sonia's lover is far more aware of his control over her than of her *vulnerability* and takes advantage of the situation when it does not go his way. This case shows how the ethic of care – understood as a model of moral development for women (Gilligan 1982) – creates constraints on women's sexual practices, encouraging them to put men's desire first and reinforcing women's primary responsibility for care. The ethic of care, for which women alone are responsible, weighs on their shoulders and makes them bend. In this respect, Sonia's role as the child's primary caregiver in maintaining these unequal relationships is significant. Sonia allows herself to be overwhelmed by her partner's desires supported by the prejudice that men have stronger desires than the women in her life. In this case, this prejudice is a defense that constrains her use of sexuality by heightening her perceived *vulnerability* and by extending her fear to encompass apprehension for children and others, and it prevents her to recognize her physical and psychological limits. Yet it is crucial to create a space of one's own. It is essential to the blossoming of desire in the relationship. Otherwise, it can be reasonably argued that if this condition is not met, the defensive gender ideologies (virility and muliebrity) colonize the psychic processes mobilized in the amorous encounter.

1.8 Create a space for play where female desire can flourish

Fortunately, as Franzi's experience shows, the ethic of care suggests possibilities for reducing fear and enhancing safety for women within the BDSM communities by extending care beyond the individual. Women's experiences of public space frequently involve giving or receiving care or reinforcing relationships with friends and family. Given the remaining negative view of BDSM, it is understandable that it is important for people who practice BDSM to get closer to people in the field. Indeed, Franzi and Jasmin lost their contact with people who were very dear to them, the latter having broken the bond of friendship that united them after having learned their BDSM practices:

> It's hard to build contacts with people. They want to know, they're curious, and they ask questions, but then it's not the same … they see you in a different light, it just changes something, and that's not a good feeling. I made a friend, who I met through the kids. We were very close, she was an interesting woman, not stupid. And once the conversation was about sex and I don't know and I told her I'd rather live it than read about it. I don't know…. And she looked at me strangely and after that our friendship soon faded away…. I don't know if it had anything to do with it, maybe she thought it was weird.

Thus, the use of the BDSM communities is an opportunity to sustain relationships, which generates important benefits at individual, social, and political levels. Women's engagement in the BDSM scene is the opportunity to establish relationships with other dominant women and can be seen as another possibility of empowerment. Interaction with dominant women in the public realm, exchange on *FetLife* groups, and mail exchange are recognized and valued facets of their sexual life. Such relationships are seen as vital by many women, like Franzi, as a way to avoid madness:

> I need these people like a family. I need that. When my child was born 6, 7 years ago I had no contact with people from the scene…. Because it was too complicated. We didn't have grandparents here. We couldn't really go out. We were just completely normal people together. Then I started thinking I'm going crazy. After 5, 6 years I told Chris we have to stop doing this. I have to get back to my environment, I have to see my family again. I need more people around me … this BDSM world.

In their use of this space between women, women provide care for themselves through, for example, exchange of tips, recreation, retreat, and education, exchange of assistance, and sharing gifts with others. Interview respondents frequently described using public spaces to "feel at home" or "feel safe."

Jasmin accuses patriarchal society of preventing women from "breathing" and feeling comfortable, safe, and able to live out their sexuality as dominant women in the BDSM scene. Women like Jasmin may seek to reduce fear and eliminate danger by withdrawing from interaction and caring in the BDSM scene and retreat to more intimate, semi-public playspaces.

> When I get tired of [dominating in the public sphere] I retreat into my private sphere. One foot in the scene and one foot in the private sphere, when the scene gets too heady, then I get out. The problem is that there are few dominant women, not because women are not dominant in their sexuality, but because society takes them for "bitches" or hysterical if they behave like that.

Moreover, at the beginning there are extremely many submissive men, who impose their will. This is a big problem that women face. On the one hand you are dominant, on the other hand you are just a woman in a patriarchal society. And it totally clashes. The dominant men, when they see that you are a dominant woman, try to be more dominant than you. It's like a competition to dominate. And it's tiring. I don't want that. And that's the two problems we have in the scene. In this stupid patriarchal society, dominant women are disturbing. That's why there are very few places where you can be dominant. That's why I do parties where there are only submissive men and dominant women, because in a private space men are not so invasive, because it's small, if one starts to cause a problem right away, he won't have to deal with a woman, but with most of them, that's why we can break the system a bit. That's why I do it, it's more pleasant for the dominant women.

Her testimony suggests that a cleavage between a sphere where female domination would be practiced in an intimate circle and the public sphere is necessary for women's enjoyment of public space activity, which, in turn, implies the creation and strengthening of sustainable social ties.

1.9 Conclusion

Care work occupies a central place in the construction of BDSM sexuality where women dominate. In this respect, the BDSM communities are indebted to the work of professional dominatrixes. The interviewees reveal the intersection of commercial and non-commercial practices in daily life in their affective, material, and psychological dimensions. The care work of professional dominatrixes plays an important role in the submissive male–female dominant relationship. This is the aspect most emphasized in popular culture. In fact, films about female domination often portray **professional** female domination. It is this representation of female domination that is given so often that it does not seem that other forms of female domination exist. The near monopoly exercised by commercial female domination tends to essentialize it, to make it disappear, and thus to invisibilize its importance in contemporary BDSM culture. Although pop songs, movies, and TV shows form the "public" material of our fantasies (de Lauretis 2007), in both material and conceptual terms, the relation between the act of love and work for money isn't reflected on.

The analysis of the sadistic practices of the interviewees highlights the continuum of the sexual service of professional dominatrixes and care work (Boris and Parrenas 2010). Nurses, home-care workers, professional dominatrixes, cleaners, aides, and educators share common attributes. Each of these forms of labor forges interdependent relations and represents work assumed to be the unpaid or badly paid responsibility of women and more specifically by women from a lower class or racial outsiders. Thus, special attention should be paid to the continuity that exists between the organization of work and the erotic economy of bodies. The body of the submissive is the body that cries wanting the attention of his mummy, blushes in front of a severe school teacher, or trembles in front of the injections of a sadistic nurse. In comparison, the body of the dominatrix crumbles under the inopportune demands of the others, bends under the weight of social injections, and ultimately finds it hard to breathe sailing in a universe where her pleasure is inaudible.

By emphasizing the notion of work and suffering at work, the argument that women have less sexual drive than men is much more difficult to hold. The fact that there are fewer dominant women can be explained by several constraints including limited resources (money), responsibilities (care work), and restrictive gender norms (whore stigma). The impact of such constraints was confirmed in interviews with women about their use of BDSM communities. Those constraints for women's use of public space can be understood in the context of unequal repartition of care. How can one explain that BDSM protocols have remained so timid about considering the distribution of power relations in BDSM ethics? I think that it is because if the relationship to care, through erotic games and fetishes, were recognized as the main source of pleasure, the patriarchal ideology that motivates the unequal social distribution of care work and the devalued and invisibilized work of care givers would have to be recognized as an accessory to their erotic appeal. Neither the systematic adoption of care work in games of female domination (in games of feminization of the maids for instance) nor the excitement associated with it could be explained. Thus, we can also understand this avoidance as a defense against the risk to which the practitioners of female domination expose themselves: that their mode of sexual satisfaction no longer works, that they feel a less intense, less explosive pleasure. The relationship between suffering and drive is closer than it seems. Suffering and drive find a common denominator in work, on the one hand, and in the body, on the other. The strength of this relationship is observable through the defensive ideologies of gender developed in the work (virility and muliebrity) mobilized in the intimacy as well as in their subversion in the fantasies and sexual practices of sexual domination. My interviews reveal that the sexual division of labor persists. Family responsibilities and domestic chores still fall mostly on women's shoulders. Unfortunately, under these conditions, defensive gender ideologies (virility and muliebrity) colonize the psychic processes mobilized in the amorous encounter. It is then essential to put in place strategies to fight against these inequalities that make it extremely difficult to exercise these practices in a consensual and creative way.

Note

1 https://imgur.com/a/tLcWL

Bibliography

Altman D. (2001). *Global Sex*. Chicago, IL, The University of Chicago Press.
Boris E., Parrenas R. S. (2010). *Intimate Labors: Cultures, Technologies, and the Politics of Care*. Stanford, CA, Stanford University Press.

Buffault A. V. (1991). *The History of Tears: Sensibility and Sentimentality in France*. Hound-mills, Basingstoke, Hampshire, Macmillan.

De Lauretis T. (2007). *Théorie queer et culture populaires. De Foucault à Cronenberg*. Paris, La dispute coll. "Le genre du monde", traduit par Marie-Hélène Bourcier.

De M'Uzan M. (1951). *Inhibition, symptôme et angoisse*, 137. Paris, PUF.

Foucault A. (1994). *Françoise Maîtresse*. Paris, Gallimard.

Fur G. (2004). *Osez tout savoir sur le SM*. Paris, La Musardine.

Gilligan C. (1982). *In a Different Voice: Psychological Theory and Women's Development*. Cambridge, MA, Harvard University Press.

Goodin R. E. (1985). *Protecting the Vulnerable: A Reanalysis of Our Social Responsibilities*. Chicago, IL, University of Chicago Press.

Graham Scott G. (1997). *Erotic Power: An Exploration of Dominance and Submission*. New York, Citadel.

Hart L. (2003). *La performance sadomasochiste: Entre corps et chair*. Paris, EPEL.

Hochschild A. R. (1983). *The Managed Heart: Commercialization of Human Feeling*. California, University of California.

Illouz E. (2012). *Pourquoi l'amour fait mal. L'expérience amoureuse dans la modernité*. Paris, Seuil.

Kimmel M. S. (2005). *The History of Men. Essays on the History of American and British Masculinities*, 32. Albany, SUNY Press.

Laugier S. (2010). L'éthique du care en trois subversions. *Multitudes*, 42(3), 112–125.

McCarthy J., Edwards R., Gillies V. (2003). *Making Families: Moral Tales of Parenting and Step-Parenting*. Durham, NC, Sociology Press.

Molinier P. (2000). Virilité défensive, masculinité créatrice. *Travail, genre et sociétés*, 3(1), 25–44.

Molinier P. (2006). *Les enjeux psychiques du travail*. Paris, Petite Bibliotheque Payot.

Molinier P., Laugier S., Paperman P. (2009). *Qu'est-ce que le care. Souci des autres, sensibilité, responsabilité*. Paris, Petite Bibliotheque Payot.

Nussbaum M. (2006). La littérature comme philosophie morale. In S. Laugier (dir.), *Ethique, littérature, vie humaine*. Paris, PUF.

O'Nomis A. (2013). *The History and Arts of the Dominatrix*. Ebooks, Collector's edition ebook.

Rubin G. (1984) 1992. Thinking sex: Notes from a radical theory of the politics of sexuality. In C. S. Vance (Ed.), *Pleasure and Danger: Exploring Female Sexuality*, 267–319. London, Pandora Press.

Rubin G. (2001). *Surveiller et Jouir: Anthropologie Politique du Sexe*. Paris, Epel.

Scott G. G. (2014). *Erotic Power. An Exploration of Dominance and Submission*. Secaucus, NJ, Citadel.

Tronto J. (1993). *Moral Bounderies: A Political Argument for an Ethic of Care*. New York, Routledge.

Varrin C. (2004). *Female Dominance: Rituals and Practices*. New York, Citadel Press.

Weinberg T., Kamel G. W. Levi., (Eds.). (1983). *S and M: An Introduction to the Study of Sadomasochism*. New York, Prometheus Books.

Series and Movies

Ackeren, R. van (1983). *Die Flambierte Frau*, D. Geissier Filmprod, Deutschland.

Dick K. (1996). *Sick: The Life and Death of Bob Flanagan: Supermasochist*. Cinepix, Film Properties.

Flanagan B. (1994). *Visiting Hours: An Installation by Bob Flanagan in Collaboration with Sheree Rose*. New York, New Museum of Contemporary Art.

Lance S. (2014). *My Mistress*, Mini Studios, Australia.

Polanski R. (2013). *La Vénus à la fourrure*, R. B. Production/A. S. Film, France.

Schroeder B. (1975). *Maîtresse*, Pierre Andrieux, France.

Treut M. (1983). *Verführung: Die grausame Frau*, René Gundelach, Deutschland, 1985.

2

WORKING AS A PROFESSIONAL DOMINATRIX

2.1 Introduction

My research on female domination led me to the salons of female domination where I started an immersion survey through the questions that I asked myself about my subject and the material difficulties that one encounters as a student. My material focuses on my immersion in a dominatrix salon in Brandenburg, where I did a four-month internship. It, therefore, focuses on the activity of sex workers who do not offer genital sex but rather a range of paid sexual services, from foot fetishes to role-playing or sodomy with a strap-on dildo. I defend here the thesis that professional dominatrixes, through this paid service, propose a particular form of care where they exercise their sadism to enhance their client's pleasure.

Sadism is a motor of the investment in work and is not reducible to the sphere of sexual work assumed exclusively by dominatrixes. According to Molinier, sadism is a driving force in the investment in work. It is necessary to manage its drive, in order to do its work well, which is to relieve the suffering (Molinier 2006: 67). That being said, it is obviously more explicit within the framework of a contractualized and commercialized exchange where the dominatrix must express her sadism. She must manage not to give in to it and to sublimate it in the precision of the practices of domination by giving a sufficient dose of pain so that it is felt by the customer but avoiding it being too strong, allying effectiveness and research of the pleasure of the customer. Levey noted earlier that the work of dominatrixes complicates our understanding of the emotional labor of sex workers because "unlike other sex workers who often have to feign interest and flirtation to make their clients feel wanted, the dominatrix is asked to act out emotions like indifference and disgust" (Levey and Pinsky 2015a: 438). My analysis in the psychodynamics of work reveals the importance of considering the

DOI: 10.4324/9781003258537-4

contradictions of acting out expressions such as indifference and disgust while expressing personality traits related to compassion and care. Understanding the work of the dominatrixes and the factors to be taken into account to evaluate a session implies an analysis of the zeal of the dominatrixes. Improvisation, ingenuity, tricks, and the invention of procedures are mobilized at each moment to solve difficult situations so that "the show goes on."

From a psychological point of view, dominatrixes must execute a "double task," which is a double psychic investment called emotional work (Hochschild 1983). The repertoire of techniques used, the working habits of the dominatrixes, the technical sensitivity mobilized, and the mastery of the situation and of the body of the submissive at work is like a perilous juggling exercise. What psychological and social resources are mobilized to defend against the risks of emotional exhaustion? What strategies of distancing are put in place in situations where paid work and sexual life are in great continuity, which is the case when women who have a sexuality with a submissive in their private life practice domination in a professional way like Katerina with whom I worked? This will be highlighted through the articulation of professional and personal times in the perspective of care.

The impregnation by the preoccupation of work is useful as the time to reflect on past problems helps to anticipate future problems. But it also tends to jeopardize the possibilities to get away from work, to relax, and to devote oneself to other things. Thus, the subjective time of work is never lived passively but is the object, in the psychological register, of attempts to control it in order to defend oneself from its outbursts and try to contain them. These conflicts are difficult to resolve, especially for people who are socially isolated. In this respect, I will discuss, in particular, the consequences caused by the "whore stigma," by which sex workers who embody the ultimate breach of culturally acceptable sexual behavior for women (Rubin 1984) are especially affected. While the defenses mobilized to fight the whore stigma in the construction of the identity of dominatrixes are central, the psychic cost of this stigmatization for dominatrixes is staggering.

2.2 The sexual work of dominatrixes in a domination salon in Berlin: a space between traditional femininity and resistance

The scientific interest alone is not enough to explain my immersion in the salons of domination. In 2012, I had been living in Berlin for about a year, in a pretty precarious situation, surviving with odd jobs, for a salary of less than 800 euros per month. It was in this context that a man with whom I was chatting regularly as part of the research slipped the following idea into my ear: "Why don't you do domination sessions in a studio?" Since sex work is legal in Germany, why not? Legalization means that the state decriminalizes and officially regulates an act: the offense is removed from the criminal law, and regulations are imposed with two goals: protecting participants and controlling their behavior.[1]

That being said, even if prostitution is legal, it remains taboo. Having spent time with dominatrixes both inside and outside of domination parlors or dungeons, I learned that many of them do not accept having sex with clients. Then, I rationalized my fear by telling myself that there would be no penetration and that no one would touch me. I sent a very naive message to dungeons and dominatrix studios that said, "I am a doctoral student in psychology. I am doing my thesis on female domination, would you need an assistant?" To my surprise, Katerina contacted me. Her husband said afterward that he thought I was lying about being a student. He thought that saying I was a psychologist and was doing a PhD "was part of my domina persona." I realized that presenting myself in this way, "intellectually," in front of the clients was not only not a problem, but it also added value to my seduction. On the part of the dominatrixes, my presence as a "shrink" did not bother them and perhaps even reinforced their representation of practices linked to female domination as separate from prostitution and related to psychotherapy. Indeed, many dominant women define themselves as sexual therapists, sadotherapists,[2] and sex therapists, and some of them moreover put forward their training as psychologists in order to gain legitimacy (by approaching the care functions classically assigned to women).

Mistress Katerina, a pseudonym she used for work, booked an appointment for me one afternoon in her salon in the chic suburbs of Berlin. The dominatrix uses a name that is not just a pseudonym but also a stage name and an alter ego. It protects her anonymity and real-life identity, while at the same time, it allows her to live out a super version of herself and develop her dominatrix identity.

> Frequent titles include Mistress, Maîtresse, Herrin or Lady, formal title of madame Miss, Ms or od domina, Goddess, Empress, Queen. The names that were chosen often have a flavor of the feminine mystical, exotic, or foreign elements, and an accent of power.
>
> *(O'Nomis 2013: 2704)*

"The capitalization of the first letter of Dominatrix is an important element of her address, sound and written qualities of their name are examined in detail." I was Lady Gabrielle, and besides, we called each other by these first names so that the customers would get used to using them.

The following week, Katerina called me back, and I went to her house to take pictures that she could put on her website. She put in the big plan on the site a text of the style "Gabrielle, the cat" with the ravaging photos in sexy revanchist style as in *Kill Bill*. In general, all the sites of dominas swarm with selling formulas, in order to attract the greatest number of customers. An American woman who worked at another studio told me that her profile read "fresh from Texas." Dominatrixes search for "a self in her adopted style, her photographic image and writing in self-expression and self-promotion, in which they may emphasize particular interests and skills, and draws clients into her web." Their style denotes a certain kind of emphasis within their role and practices. Within the role "is something of a mystic and an expert of the psychosexual realm". In constructing her style, "a Dominatrix may look to mythology, to characters from literature and film to names" (O'Nomis 2013: 2705/3631). Moreover, the clichés that represent the dominant woman in the media play an important role in the professional world. The other woman working with Katerina, Rita, had dyed her hair black to appear more dominant. It is about being "a fantasy." I saw a certain contradiction in complying with the injunctions of sexuality where the woman appears to be a prey, playing with the male voyeurism, while practicing sexuality where this same woman wants to be dominant. Instead, professional dominance and S/M can be seen as a performance that mimics traditional gender dynamics at the same time that it upends them (Lindemann 2011).

The dominatrix's living room was located on the second floor of her house. Katerina was about 45 years old, of average height and stature, brunette, dressed all in leather, directive, not the type to radiate her smile to put you at ease. We went upstairs to the living room to talk. The space that she had arranged on the floor above was reserved for her customers. There was a living room with a piano where she first received her clients. Next to it was a dressing room. "Most Dominatrixes keep a substantial wardrobe both for themselves and for their clients" (O'Nomis 2013: 2621/3631). This includes elements of lingerie, hosiery, stiletto shoes, fetish boots, fetish garments in latex and leather, costumes for role play, an area of makeup, and jewelry. This gives an idea about the most common forms of equipment used by dominatrixes in practicing their realm arts.

Next to this room was the dungeon. "That is the most ubiquitous form of professional playspace for a dominatrix" (O'Nomis 2013: 2513/3631). The term refers to the fantasy environment of simulated imprisonment, in which the dominatrix holds her client captive and at her mercy. It is part theater and part workspace. Some dominatrixes choose to emphasize the dramatic *mise-en-scène* as an esthetic backdrop, with instruments like a throne chair that allows them to sit above a sub in status and power. But Katerina takes a pragmatic approach to the space as a workshop of trade tools, a bondage table, and a whipping bench. Like most dominatrixes, she has a range of corporal punishment equipment, derived from historical punishment purposes and from animal training. These include whips, floggers, canes, paddles, straps, tawse, riding crops, and nipple clamps. Nipple clamps are one of the most common items put to erotic use and simulated torture, which are often paired with weights also used on male genitalia at the base of the testicles. The psychological aspect of play is emphasized through the use of psychiatric restraint equipment like bench restraints.

A small room is dedicated to the practices of sensory deprivation. This "cupboard" is a piece of furniture used to imprison a captive in a small space with psychological intensity and deprive him of his sense of sight, hearing, and so forth. An element of this effect is the dark cocoon or womb-like experience of sensory deprivation, which may be amplified. Gas masks placed on a shelf allow participants to realize this sensory experience.

Like many dominatrixes, she has a special medical room in her playspace. This reflects both fantasy nurses and medical scenarios, which emphasizes the sense of bodiliness and provides an examination and procedure bench and a clinical sterile area for play. Instruments used include enema kits, sterile needles, and dildos. This room was also used as a bathroom where clients showered after the session.

At the end of the hallway, there was a "weird" seat with a hole for the head of the submissive. I asked her what it was, and she explained to me it was for the caviar, which is a cute little name for practices with feces. That said, given the taboos surrounding scatological practices, including in the BDSM milieu, the clients who indulge in them are ready to pay a lot of money for this service (250 euros on average in 2017), which explains why it is offered in many salons and why they arrange to have at least one dominatrix who offers this service.

Next door there was a hairdressing salon commonly called the "boudoir" equipped with wigs, makeup, and jewelry. Katerina has an open mind regarding all gender identities. People with a desire for cross-dressing often come and book a session in this area. She enforced forced feminization and cross-dressing or mixing male and female elements.

Like most craft dominatrixes, she has some form of suspension point. These are arranged in this boudoir there. A St. Andrew's cross, which forms an X, is also in this room at the entrance.

Katerina's story invalidates the cliché that dominatrixes have been trained in psychology. Katerina did not receive a high level of education, and although she is currently living in a luxurious house, she comes from a modest background. Her parents are migrants of Greek origin. Before becoming a professional dominatrix, Katerina was a hairdresser, which explains the hair salon, an unusual space in which she did hairdressing, makeup, and feminized clients. As Julia O'Connell Davidson argues, many sex workers' decisions are based on the limited options available to them, especially if they have few skills and access to only low-paying jobs (O'Connell Davidson 1998). My experience confirms what Teela Sanders, Maggie O'Neill, and Jane Pitcher have said: people with traditional skills, qualifications, and resumes in the workplace make rational choices to enter the sex industry in order to earn more money in less time (Sanders et al. 2009). Rationally, earning minimum wage for part-time work is less advantageous than working four times a month in a dominatrix salon for higher pay. During her first marriage, Katerina did all the housework until she met a client in her hair salon with a foot fetish who noticed her because of her high-heeled boots. When she saw how much this man did for her compared to her husband, she divorced him and decided to make female domination her profession. So it's not just the financial interest that is at stake, but the care dimension also plays an important role for Katerina. This contrasts with the common perception of the relationship between client and prostitute as marked by violence. Katerina dreams of another possible masculinity, one that is more concerned with the other, and more attentive to her desires. In this sense, female domination, such as it is invested by certain dominating women, reinterprets the scheme of courtly love.[3] Katerina fantasizes about having a man at service. It is a desire for care that she expresses – care explicitly realized by a man for a woman, an expression that I borrow from Molinier about Marguerite Duras's *L'Amant*, and which "detaches care from the maternal, installs it and eroticizes it in adult heterosexual relations, in contrast to what the psychoanalytical clinic suggests, where the truly tender and maternal man is often experienced by his partner as emasculated" (Molinier 2006: 31).

2.3 The organization of work

2.3.1 Prescribed work

Types of female domination work in Germany include the escort sector, donjons and domina studios, home-based work (up to three workers may work together legally in a residence), and BDSM clubs whose hostesses engage in sex work. The way in which dominatrixes operate is directly linked to jurisdictional law and its enforcement. In places where sex work is legal, like in Germany, dominatrixes either work from a large dungeon establishment or have the freedom to set up their own business from their home. As employers, owners of erotic businesses like Katerina have the right to set work hours, prices, and other standards of conduct norms. The situation is more complex in other countries where prostitution laws penalize the client such as France. However, for dominatrixes like Axelle de Sade, if it is possible to declare oneself officially as a sex worker, it is not advisable to do so because, with the penalization of the clients, declaring a turnover puts the sex worker and her clients in danger. Moreover, according to her, with the hardening of the laws or the possible modifications of these laws that a repressive government could bring, it is better to remain hidden. This explains why many dominatrixes claim to be masseuses, therapists, and coaches of all kinds.

By analyzing the prescribed organization of work of Katerina, I quickly understand the importance of BDSM protocols such as SSC (Safe, Sane, Consensual), RACK (Risk-Aware Consensual Kink), and 4Cs (Caring, Communication, Consent, and Caution) that separate them from cases of abuse and violence.

Before I met Katerina, I had a previous experience at a bar where there were no customers, and I did not go back because the dominatrix scared me. One described a way of working that did not correspond to any protocol. "I do BDSM like the Marquis de Sade," she said, expressing her sadism without concern for others. She affirmed that in case of an accident, when the man arrived at the hospital, the doctors would not ask more questions to the injured man, knowing how to identify the practices according to the injured organs. I can affirm that the working conditions of this dominatrix are not the norm. While the prescribed organization of work differs in these types of work, my experience in the variety of places I did a trial day confirms that all dominatrixes refer to a common protocol. The practices performed are usually listed on a website's long A to Z list of areas and activities which they cater for, listing every kind of practice and fetish. Dominatrixes who have accumulated experiences in another area can focus on a niche within a niche. Katerina, for instance, has trained as a hairdresser and has the equipment to cater to clients who enjoy this service.

The work is pretty well organized. Katerina prepares her salon in the morning for clients. She cleans everything again. "Cleanliness is vital in this kind of business. Everything has to be spotless. Shine." She receives her clients in the salon, regulars or not, about 15 minutes before the start of the session to see what's new in their lives and to inquire about what they want. For the new clients, she discusses with them based on a questionnaire on their practices, preferences, and taboos that can be downloaded or that the clients bring. She will also refuse or modify a particular form of play in consideration of a person's medical conditions, medication, fitness level, and age and mitigate risk wherever possible: "I take responsibility for this man at this moment. He comes healthy in my room. He goes back healthy [(*caring about*)]."

She sets limits: "there are limits, they are being set beforehand and followed carefully." Setting boundaries is necessary because as trust is so important in BDSM play, dominatrixes hold themselves to a level of behavior and judgment that foster trust (*caring about*).

The client's limitations are discussed during this interview as well as what they refuse to do. It may relate to the level of pain, phobias, or the particular content that a client is not prepared to receive; for instance, certain types of humiliation may be deeply arousing and emphasize the dominant/submissive relationship for some, whereas for others it may be psychologically distressing in the extreme and trigger childhood trauma.

In order to ensure the security of her customers, Katerina sets a safe word with her client. Codeword: mercy. She also sets her limits. Some things that she refuses to do are "extreme strangulation endangering the client's life," role play with the client "like the one being hanged by an executioner," and "games with animals." "Some customers innocently ask if they can come with their dog, she jokes. No way!"

Thus, she actively sets her limits for her clients and evaluates theirs on different physical, emotional, and relational levels, and their multiple relationships maintained with fantasies. "Some identify as submissive, slave, masochist, sissy or identification but some others just don't want to be identified at all." Like most dominatrixes, she pays *attention* to these nuances and "provides an open mind and space to explore a wide range of identity, desires, and needs" (O'Nomis 2013: 1375).

These discussions before the beginning of the sessions take place in a relaxed atmosphere with classical music, red wine, and often Sekt to make the client feel comfortable. Many professional dominatrixes I spoke to were surprised that alcohol is allowed. As Inanna Justice stated, "For most Dommes that I know, it's only afterwards that we'll drink alcohol together. Before the session, it's Perrier or tea." It is also during this preliminary interview that the money transaction takes place. The basis was 200 euros for a one-hour session, which corresponded to luxury escorting. Speaking of money, I liked the fact that she always arranged for the clients to give me a little something when I assisted her at the beginning.

She often gave me 50 euros at the end of the session. Katerina took the money and put it in a nice box in wood on one end of the table. The regulars and "educated" men put the money directly into this box without Katerina having to mention the money (the rates are on the website). If I continued to work for her, I would get 60% of the total amount.

My beginnings in the field are extremely different from those of Katerina. To train as a professional dominatrix took her a year, and she invested money to pay for her training led by an experienced professional dominatrix where she assisted her in sessions, in many ways, passing the other dominatrix instruments, for example, observing what was going on and learning the rules of the profession. It was only over time, as she became more and more involved in co-leading the sessions, that she participated in the slave demeanor games, the psychological power play, and the use of techniques. These skills are acquired during the training. As she often told me, this training is essential in learning how to structure the session and manage the room. This transmission of heritage arises from being able to do the work "according to the art." Her mentor taught her how to be sovereign and confident, knowing how to evaluate the result of her personal activity (*competence*). This training period, however, is not the norm, or at least if it was, it is not anymore. I had the opportunity to do a trial session in a dungeon in Berlin where I had applied. Unlike Katerina, the young woman I accompanied, who was previously working as a cashier, had not undergone any training except for the period of training (*Einarbeitung*) of the donjons.

For Katerina, when the session is over, the clients get dressed and take a shower in the bathroom. Towels are at their disposal. Katerina brings back their shoes and clothes at the exit. This notion of service is expected from the client (*caring for*). In addition to the domination service offered in Katerina's salon, an entertainment service is provided at the end of the session in the salon, where she goes back over the things that happened during the session to find out what was more appealing to the client and offers a service of listening often to their private problems by showing signs of interest in the lives of people to retain the clients. For example, Katerina listened at the end of a session where I had assisted the difficulties of a client with his partner with whom he had a distant relationship. By showing empathy and *caring for* clients, Katerina not only makes them feel special but also makes them want to have a relationship with her.

On the side of the dominatrixes I met, the enjoyment is not on the physical side but on the psychic side (Katerina spoke about *Kopfkino*: making a movie in the head). The pleasure is linked to the staging, the execution of acts, and the fact of directing a scene, setting up a scenario with activities where they are in a position of initiative and direction. An intrapsychic conflict is played out between sadistic pleasure and altruism. The dominatrix has to put aggressive drives to work in a way that is favorable to the overall mission of serving as a dominatrix, combining two qualities, that is, being dominant and remaining sovereign. It is according to these two qualities that Katerina judged my performance. At the end of the sessions, she asked the clients "how did he find me," that is, if I had played the game well, if I had been dominant, and if I had been "sovereign." Katerina told me several times, "to be a domina you have to be sovereign," that is to say, "to keep control of the situation" (*competence*). During the first sessions, I was a little afraid, but the wine, which was present at all the sessions, calmed my anxiety. I certainly took another glass. Besides, she had told an "extremely masochistic" friend to come by with some wine. Indeed, he rang the doorbell with two bottles within the hour. The man was extremely submissive and above all passive; he said nothing, waiting for Katerina to ask him questions to answer. She wanted to know how I managed the sessions with a foot fetishist and what he thought of me, so she made me go to the other room with him, the one dedicated to torture. I took off my boots and pushed my feet into his mouth, gently, and then redirected his tongue to my toes. After a while, Katerina came into the room. We had been there for more than half an hour. Apparently, she had told him to stay only 15 minutes. She scolded him because, according to her, he had done it on purpose when he knew exactly what 15 minutes meant and he had abused my time. She gave him lashes, and then finally she asked him how the session went and if, of course, I had been dominant. He told her it was fine, that I had been sovereign, and when asked if I had been dominant, he looked hesitantly and didn't state yes or no. I was stunned. We had been together for 40 minutes, him at my feet insisting on having my toe in his mouth, but now he was sizing me up. I looked at Katerina and then asked her what she meant by being dominant, in the end. She stood up and ordered him to lick her boots, adding to the insults with strokes of the whip because he was not licking in the right place. After a few minutes, she stopped and said to me: this is the foot fetish session! I looked at the man and asked him: "[B]ut is this what you want by going to a domina?" He nodded, and I had trouble understanding. I tried to explain to Katerina my point of view, I found that too theatrical, and then Katerina cut me off, saying, "[T]his is the foot fetish session, that's how it happens." I thought it lacked spontaneity, but she insisted on the fact that in order to be dominant, you have to control the session. I realized later what it means: to foresee, to organize, to structure, and in other words, to correct reality so that it bends to your will and thus reduce uncertainty.

At the beginning of each session, Katerina put on a CD. A session did not exceed the duration of the music on one side of the CD. But often domination sessions ended at the moment of ejaculation. Katerina offered a masturbation service to the client. The wish that the session ends with the client's ejaculation is not shared by all dominatrixes. Although Katerina considered that the work should end with the client's ejaculation, her colleague did not want to provide this service and asked the clients who came to her to masturbate once they got home. We can make the hypothesis that the erection is inhibited by fear and by the desire to do well, to please the dominatrix. But above all, I have understood over time that people do not come for that, but they are looking for other bodily sensations not related to genital sexuality. This desire on Katerina's part to make her clients come can be explained by the fact that the latter, as Eric Bidaud notes, is "the index of knowledge and constitutes a partial truth" (Bidaud 2016). In his study inviting psychoanalysis to examine porn, basing himself on the course of Foucault in *Subjectivity and Truth*, he writes, "There is in the pleasure, what affects the body, the idea given to the subject that something true happens," and further, he adds that there is the idea "of a concordance body/significant" (Boehringer and Foucault 2015). The venal domination, in the living room of Katerina, revalorizes the aspects of genital heterosexuality in BDSM practices. Yet, even though ejaculation may be valued, sexuality in heterosexual BDSM lounges shows mostly aspects of non-genital heterosexuality.

2.3.2 Beyond the prescribed, the real

By analyzing the prescribed organization of work, one can know who does what and how, who is responsible for the sessions, with what tools are they conducted, according to what protocol, in how much time, according to what evaluation criteria, etc. But my work in the field and the confrontation with clients in concrete situations have made me understand that the knowledge of dominatrixes is founded and elaborated in the active interaction with the situations of professional domination, and it is the result of practice and is learned in action, that is to say, precisely everything that happens beyond this reassuring framework. "Knowledge based on feeling is not only based on acquired theoretical – or rather cognitive – knowledge, it is elaborated in active interactivity with the environment, it is the result of practice and it is learned in action" (Molinier 2006: 109).

The relationship with the environment is the basis of a sympathetic trade with objects and people based on empathy and subjective involvement. To be credible in the role of dominatrix, some accessories like high heels and fishnet stockings are essential. This manufactured, modified, improved costume helps her to identify with the dominant woman she represents and to start her domination sessions. For many dominatrixes, these accessories are essential. Indeed, as Katerina told me,

> [S]ometimes I am not in the mood to play. Sometimes you're in a bad mood, you've had some bad news, you don't feel like being sexy, making yourself beautiful, and playing out fantasies, representing that fantasy, being another person. Strangely enough, from the moment I put on my makeup and my uniform, strangely enough, something turns around in my mind and I am Mistress Katerina.

She changes between herself and her dominatrix role like a mask worn and shed. With time, she develops her own style and embodies more this role of dominatrix. These masks, costumes, and jewelry become integral parts of the body, and the body transcends itself, exceeds, and merges with the person. She takes the traits and the appearance of a powerful woman that resonate with her and fashion her dominatrix identity in a manner that is consciously attuned to male desire. This relationship between the world of work and the tools of work echoes Michel Henry's concept of bodypropriation (corpspropriation) (Henry 1965). According to him, the appropriation of one's body would pass by the engagement in the work. The body of which is in question is not the biological body, but it is the body that one lives, that feels affectively, that is engaged in the relation with the other, and that designates the erotic body in psychoanalysis. It is from this body that a self-transformation can take place. Katerina testifies that the performance of dominatrix she had to play for her clients has transformed her personality. She says that she is more determined, domineering, and direct in her relationships with others without really trying to be, but her work demands it of her. Indeed, the place of work in the psychic life exceeds largely the limits of the time of the official, contractual work – working in a mutative process that does not only transform the world by producing service for the client but also transform herself by working.

In describing Katerina's sex work, it is difficult to generalize about a dominatrix's activities, as the degree of sexual intimacy maintained with clients is far from uniform. As she explained to me, intimacy depends on the situation and varies according to the type of social connection with the client. Intimacy with a club regular would not be the same as with a "real friend." I saw this through her relationship with a client who came four times a month. I think he started talking about his health problems when he arrived, and Katerina got angry after a while and said curtly that she didn't want to hear about that. It was really hard, and I was uncomfortable. This dryness was more likely with the "real boyfriend" because there are real feelings of tenderness. At the same time, the degree of intimacy that she maintains with his masochistic friends is not uniform, because the beauty of men, their kindness, talent, and services rendered increase the probability of erotic interactions.

In intimate relationships with unknown people, dominatrixes have to have a flair for not putting themselves in danger. Dominatrixes actively determine their boundaries by refusing certain clients who are requesting certain sexual acts that they don't feel like performing like I mentioned above and by refusing clients whom they can't trust. Katerina told me that after opening her door and seeing one of the clients, she immediately asked him to leave and contact other dominatrixes trusting her intuition. "I need to be able to look at myself in the mirror again in the morning," she confided to me. As O'Neill has already pointed out, performing the role of the prostitute requires exceptional control of the inner world in order to survive as a sex worker (O'Neill 2001). This includes questioning the limits one can afford to set for oneself. This includes asking yourself what boundaries you can afford to violate without disturbing your inner world. It also includes learning to avoid potentially violent clients whose inner world would be unmanageable.

This sensitive perception is essential to the realization of domination sessions. It participates intrinsically in the qualification of the dominatrix as dominant and sovereign (*competence*). Thus, beyond the prescribed work, there is the real. The real work here is the mastery of all that is not controllable: the live sessions, the events to come, the differences of personalities between colleagues and customers, the market, the competing exhibitions, the technical and technological problems, and the self-control. It makes itself known through the unexpected. The problems encountered are unprecedented. They plunge us in the disarray because they put us in front of the unknown. We did not expect it. What personally surprised me the most in the field was the discomfort of many clients with a prostitute and in this context with the "aberrations" of their sexuality. I discovered that most of the men who frequented the domination salons were afraid and that many of them had very little experience. This fear – which contrasts with the confidence with which men refer to each other as dating sex workers to reinforce their masculinity – is, however, visible through physical markers such as trembling, curling fingers, and excessive sweating. As dominatrixes, one has to deal with fear. I realize then that sadistic control is not the only psychological problem. It is about treating the body as an object, reifying it. At the same time, the dominatrix can be moved by the fear of her client or disgusted by the smell of the sweat coming out of his body, amused by the ridiculousness of certain situations, or afraid of making a mistake in front of a much older or more experienced client. These affective modalities are not in the sensitive experience dissociated from each other.

During my first interview with Katerina, she had opened a bottle of Sekt (sparkling white wine, a product of the RDA, which has survived). We had drunk two glasses when she asked me if I wanted to stay because she was waiting for a customer. This example of a session focuses attention on the acts performed and more on the individual and psychological processes of work, that is to say, on the invisible part of work – its subjective side. The man arrived on time, and he was very polite but a little tensed for this first appointment with Katerina. This client was about 50 years old and told us he was a tax inspector. A bit bald with a remnant of curly locks on the side, he was quite strong, he had the belly of men of his age well settled in their routine and started to sweat quickly, and he was not very comfortable apparently. He was smiling, but his smile looked like a nervous tic; in fact, I was struck by the fact that this man collected nervous tics. He wanted to have his hair done like a woman, and he told us an anecdote from his childhood: his aunt used to force him as a child to have a bowl cut, and he hated this hairstyle and apparently felt humiliated after having his hair done. His interpretation was that he would have internalized this trauma to then eroticize it and want to replay it. We went to the hairdressing salon where she dressed him in a black latex dress with heeled boots. Katerina looked at him sure of herself and encouraged him warmly with "wow, great, you look wonderful." She had a really sincere air, one would have almost said that she was convinced. Then she did hairdressing with the rest of the hair he had, as she was a hairdresser by training. As she went through a hairdressing apprenticeship when she was young, she was able to draw on this experience to establish her assertive dominance. As she says, a dominatrix relies on her skills to develop her persona. Thus, she was able to draw on these skills to slip into the role of a professional dominatrix and thus allow the session to begin without letting the anxiety generated by identification with the drama of this client filter through. In my opinion, this allowed her to maintain a certain emotional distance that enabled her to carry out her work. For Mistress Inanna,

> [t]his emotional distancing is vital in surviving as a Domme, or any sex worker, for that matter. On one hand, we need to create a bond with our clients to get them to come back; on the other, we need to preserve our intimate energy and learn how to give it out only in small doses that we can recuperate from quickly.

2.4 Being in the border area

Cleavage can be presented in an ordinary way to remove certain destabilizing perceptions during the work. This distancing is an element in the defensive system that allows sex workers to "hold it together" at work. They maintain to separate their two lives, they say. Mistress Sandra, for example, who forbids herself from certain things like genital sex with her submissives during the sessions, has sexual relations with her slave with whom she has been in a relationship for two years, "[b]ecause he is in my intimacy, the others are not." She tells me that she "puts a lot of boundaries between her private BDSM life and her private life." She maintains two parallel lives. This cleavage is protective of her mental health. If we follow certain psychoanalysts, perfect independence between two psychic functionings within the same subject is only possible when there is a "personality cleavage" previously inscribed in the very structure of the subject. This is what is called a perverse organization of the personality. In *Le corps d'abord*, Dejours (2001) proposes another theory of cleavage, called the theory of cleavage of the third Freudian topical. In this perspective, the cleavage can be extended to the psychic functioning as a whole, whatever the structure of the personality (with variable configurations according to the structures). Understood in this way, the cleavage is less a defense *per se* than the result of defensive processes that construct a denial of reality. For sex workers like Katerina for instance, above all the dominatrixes sell an illusion, a role play, it is *Kopfkino*. She never mentioned about her personal life while talking with clients. This distance between herself and her clients makes sure that Katerina didn't break the fantasy and also, as she said, helps her to stay sovereign. In a session where I was to assist Katerina, I wanted to talk about general problems at the workplace, but Katerina immediately interrupted me because we were not supposed to talk about our problems: "Here we are mistresses. We represent a sexual fantasy. Your personal history, your contradictions, your problems should not appear."

However, relating her experience of sexual work, Katerina highlights the permeability between different types of investments and experiences. For her, the work of dominant women is important because everything becomes mechanical in our society. People are expected to function above all else, and to meet this demand, they have to put aside their real needs. When people come to me, they ask for comfort, human warmth, and well-being. She sets up the boundary fantasies of the clients according to their script. This psychic permeability that allows the expression of personal affective experiences in the service of the quality of the care of the clients is a psychic flexibility and a form of subjective moral autonomy (Pharo 1996). To feel this degree of intimacy is ecstatic. "You are in the border area, like when you perform taboo fantasies like a brown shower" (sometimes referred to as "hard sports"). "There is something fascinating about passing between the two worlds."

However, there are things that cause emotional stress. It happens that after a session, Katerina wonders what happened/what went wrong. Sometimes she says that she needs hours to come back to earth and work on what happened during a session. This shows that it is not easy to "switch off," because a lot of work has to be done on oneself to evaluate the session and come back down. Then, this permeability has a counterpart. It can also allow the anguish generated by identification with the drama of others to filter through. "This touches on problems that are well known to carers: those of the 'right distance' to establish in order to provide good care without getting emotionally 'burnt.' In other words, we touch on the suffering-defense dynamic" (Molinier 2009). Especially, this type of work raises the question of the authenticity of one's feelings expressed and/ or felt and of the possible alienation of subjectivity exploited by the service relationship. From a psychological point of view, for women service workers, the work accomplished means a double psychic investment in what sociologists call, following Arlie Hochschild, emotional labor (Hochschild 1983). During our first interview, when Katerina asked about my experience in this field, I told that I had accumulated experience in my private life. She explained that dominating clients had nothing to do with doing it in private. She did not particularly like most of her clients, and she would not play with them if they did not pay. This is not to say that she does this only for the money. She enjoys domination and practices it in her private life with her partner. Most dominatrixes like Inanna would still do this if they were not paid. "Just statistically not with the clients that come see me." Thus, the inauthenticity of the emotions staged in sex work can go so far as to generate feelings of strangeness to oneself and distort the expression of private feelings. This is the main reason why I did not continue the experiment. I couldn't handle the authenticity of the emotions I had to put into my work and, on the contrary, I started to treat my lovers in my private life as objects of study. It became impossible for me to keep my private life and my work separate. This is consistent with my observations of sessions with Katerina. Once a client canceled at the last minute a session that Katerina was particularly looking forward to. Her excitement was then gone immediately, leaving her angry and desperate. Katerina's emotional state was in every way comparable to that of the rejected lover. In every way, I repeat, because the client in question had paid for the session in advance. If we stick to her business alone, she has lost nothing. Thus, cleavage isn't always easy to maintain all the more so as one is invested in this form of sexuality in his intimate life.

While some of the issues related to the work–life divide that dominating women face are unavoidable, restrictive gender norms tend to give them a closed and strict boundary that limits their options. Dominatrixes must manage the fine line between being in control and not crossing the boundaries imposed by the sexual double standard. Lots of clients are married as she mentioned to me. Some claim to use their services so as not to have to cheat on their wives, again, as I mentioned earlier, because of the commonly held view that if there is no penetration, it is not really cheating, as is the case with many of the clients I have met in the field. Professional dominatrixes, therefore, take care to maintain the cleavage between BDSM sexuality and the emotional and marital life of their clients. For example, it is important to know whether the man is married or not, as they are usually afraid of the body marks that the wife might discover. For Katerina, having to deal with the boundaries was one of the most difficult aspects of her job. In one interview, she mentioned a mistake she had made in one of her sessions with a married man, whom she taunted by physically dominating him by mentioning that his wife did not do that to him. The session went badly. Her tutor then taught her the rule of never mentioning marital relationships. Dominants must manage the fine line between sharing a particular moment of intimacy that is taboo in relationships and blatantly mentioning them. They must simulate intimacy while constantly doing the work of setting boundaries. This requires the development of skills, styles, and strategies of concealment. In this regard, we can see the arrogant, haughty attitude of dominatrixes not only as a selling point to attract and retain customers but also as a way to set boundaries with customers, to manage the stress associated with pressing demands. In other words it can be understood as a defense mechanism.

The mommy/whore divide (or dual sexual morality) also plays an important role in the recourse of some men to sex workers, who have vanilla sexuality with their wives or life partners and are unable to cross certain boundaries imposed by a conception of a heterosexual sexuality. As Christina mentions:

> Some submissives have a double life. They are married, and want to be fucked by a man, so they communicate their fantasy to their mistress. I have this kind of client. They don't consider themselves gay because of the taboo. They have dominas who rent them out to be fucked by men and they are super happy with that. You can tell them to go to this parking lot and give a man a blow-job or something and ask them to give you the money they earned. Basically you become a kind of pimp, and for them it's a total dream. There are websites like *Sklavenzentral* where you can offer this kind of service.

I observe especially that the cleavage of spheres, prostitution, and the taboo of homosexuality maintain a close link. This is at least suggested by the case of a client with whom I had a session, who came to be penetrated by dominas not wanting to practice this with his wife, insisting that he had no homosexual tendency. This will to deny his homosexual desires suggests that the performance of anal penetration threatens the masculinity of this masochistic man. During the session, while I was penetrating this client with a vibrator, I made the mistake of talking to him while identifying him as a submissive. He then took me back and told me that he didn't appreciate it. But the mistake was made. The reality of the encounter with me "stimulated the whole of the repressed and non-repressed unconscious, and specifically a zone of sensitivity of the unconscious described by Michel Fain, where the unconscious is stimulated by reality via perception" (Dejours 2018: 91). And when the denial is crossed, the consequences can be harmful to the dominatrix. At the end of the session, he stayed inside the shower for a while and then got impatient, came out, and asked me why I hadn't brought him his things. I learned that once the session was over, that's what the other girls did, so he took the opportunity to argue with me because I had scratched him a bit and he had a little mark. While I apologized, he lectured me in a paternalistic tone: "Be careful you know most of the men who come here are married." It was a good opportunity for him to "put things in their place" and to give himself a bit of composure. This person made me understand that some clients could wish for practices with a dominatrix while maintaining a dominant attitude that protects them from feeling assimilated to the submissive men they perceive as devirilized. Thus, shame would also play an important role in men's recourse to professional women with whom they can reaffirm their virility by exchanging money and resorting to socially despised women on the margins. The "femininity" of masochistic men is thus itself controlled in a device where the man retains his social prerogatives. To keep the control on the dominant woman, via exchange of money, seems to play like a mechanism of defense to preserve the virility "whose psychological spring resides in the shame to pass for a woman" (Molinier 2000). The taboo of the homosexuality rests on powerful mechanism projectors. The panic of this man generated by the disorder that male masochism introduces in the gender system is projected on women. Thus, in his case, the whore stigma functions like a powerful instrument in the service of heteronormativity. Indeed, it acts again the danger that these men take by having an anal sexuality. The latter being as Judith Butler says, "a transgression of the limits, a dangerous threat of pollution for the social system synecdochically represented by the body" (Butler 1990). Indeed, the anal sexuality of this customer is to take again the terms of Leo Bersani, identified "with an imaginary version of the female sexuality" (Bersani 1998: 48). In our economic context, this client can fight against this identification with women by addressing prostitutes, a population of mostly women exercising an extremely stigmatized, criticized, and blamed profession to which he does not belong, thus being able to prove that he is different from women.

2.5 Discussion

In popular culture, only the representation of professional female domination is considered. The quasi-monopoly exercised by commercial female domination tends to invisibilize its importance in the contemporary BDSM culture. But if the problem linked to the lack of recognition of sex work is to be put forward, the suffering associated with the lack of recognition is well supported when the work has a meaning (Molinier 2006). On the other hand, the suffering linked to the stigmatization of prostitution and prostitutes is omnipresent in the lives of dominatrixes. This stigma leads me, for instance, to have to conceal my professional identity. When I was working with Katerina, I was at Humboldt University at the time taking German classes to other students. If you can say that you are studying the BDSM scene, it is not possible without breaking the social bond, to say that you are a sex worker, which put me in the situation of keeping a secret and therefore feeling like I had to watch myself in the presence of teachers and students. Working as a professional dominatrix is, in fact, a job that leads to its practitioners being isolated in the long run. Most of the people in Katerina's entourage were connected to professional female domination. Working in a domination salon is a solitary job. A large part of Katerina's work consisted of waiting for the clients to call her in her apartment, who often hung up out of fear. But she also has to deal with many clients who call and hang up or cancel the session at the last minute. Alcohol has calmed the anger caused by these inconveniences and helped to reduce it.

> Alcohol plays an important role in collective defense strategies against fear. It acts as a disinhibitor, euphoriant, exciter, short-term antidepressant, anxiolytic, aphobic. Alcohol makes you feel more confident, it gives you a boost and a temporary feeling of warmth, it calms your shivers.
>
> *(Dejours 2015: 119)*

The alcohol problem should not be dissociated from a reflection on organizational constraints, the relationship to risk and fear associated with the whore stigma, and boredom. The fact that dominatrixes often live and work in a single private residence has the consequence of limiting their interactions with the community at large, minimizing contact with the outside world, and thus increasing their psychic, social, and physical vulnerabilities. The importance of the collective in its dimension of protection from danger is put forward by Inanna Justice. She organizes a monthly dinner in Paris, "Le dîner des dommes," which allows professional dominatrixes to support each other emotionally and to discuss the joys and woes of the profession, which inevitably leads to talking about safety, protecting oneself from freaks, and sharing techniques to protect oneself better. The absence of the collective contributes to a state of both physical and social isolation and can have an impact on workers' vulnerability, which can lead, among other things, to addictive behavior. Communicating and receiving information, choosing their own affiliations, and joining and leaving groups and organizations are all options and choices for dominants that play a role in their mental health. This is why Axelle de Sade is involved in the collective of sex workers in France. She highlights the advantage of being part of this organization in the sense that it allows sex workers to support each other by exchanging good practices and materials for example. She emphasizes the importance of getting organized in order to better practice her profession and better defend herself. This can be done by setting up workshops and legal or mutual services, or by sharing the list of blacklisted clients (Jasmine application developed by Médecins du Monde and STRASS). This collective is also a place of support and accompaniment for sex workers who have suffered violence (orientation toward adequate structures, support for the victims, etc.).

That being said, the status of sex workers and the associated stigma make it difficult for them to leave their jobs, especially if the person has a migration background and is discriminated in the job market. Therein the profession of a dominatrix is hardly distinguishable from that of prostitutes, who embody the ultimate breach of culturally acceptable sexual behavior for women (Rubin 1984) and are then especially affected by the whore stigma. This assimilation tends dominatrixes to produce discourses reproducing gendered stereotypes in the form of "I am not a whore," a defensive discursive formation that divides women rather than unites them. They distinguish themselves by refusing certain sexual practices with submissives, by limiting access to certain parts of their bodies, or by avoiding exposing certain parts publicly. Thus, fellatio and genital sex in a D/S relationship with a submissive are taboo. This is the same observation made by R. S. Parrenas in her study of bar hostesses in Japan. She notes that most hostesses clearly distinguish between flirting for money and having sex for money, and therefore do not equate their activity with prostitution (Parrenas 2012). This can be analyzed in retrospect as a defense mechanism that would mitigate the whore stigma. In Katerina's case, her narration in the form *I am not a prostitute* is paradoxical because she shared many codes with prostitutes. For example, she did not put her bag on the floor and told me never to do it because it was a bad sign, a sign that the clients would not come anymore. Or when she received money from a client at the end of the session, she would spit on it, believing that this supposedly brings in money. This positioning is thus particularly ambiguous, since she defends herself against being a prostitute while at the same time adopting certain codes of prostitution loudly and proudly.

The consistency of disavowing doing the work of a prostitute is reinforced by other techniques of bravado. My experience shows the influence of discourses from psychology interpreted and appropriated in such a way that they fit the dominatrixes' own designs. It appears that many dominatrixes define themselves by using terms, formulas, and concepts derived and propagated among psychologists. Expressing themselves using the jargon of psychologists allows dominatrixes to impose themselves and to find legitimacy for their conceptions of sexual relations and practices. I think not only in their name-calling (like sadotherapist), some tools used (psychiatric restraint equipment like the bench restraint), but also in taking training courses in psychology and in the way they negotiate their interactions with clients. Let's recall, as Axelle mentioned, that in countries where prostitution is illegal, sex workers declare themselves as therapists due to the hardening of the laws or possible modifications or a repressive government, preferring to remain hidden.

Inanna Justice sometimes uses analysis as part of the services she offers to people seeking to discover their fantasies and desires in relation to female domination. Symbolic representations of the psychoanalysis universe reinforce the disavowal of the whore stigma too. I think, in particular, of a scene in the film *The Venus in Furs* from Polanski (2013) where Wanda, sitting on a chair wearing glasses, is in the position of an analyst in front of the director Thomas who is lying on the sofa and sharing confidences with her.

The stigma can be disavowed, but at the tiniest misstep, displaying bad taste, the dominatrix is referred back to her abject, subaltern status. Once, for example, a client had doubts about the seriousness of the studio. Katerina became very upset and kept telling me that her salon was the most popular in Berlin as if to convince herself. In a state of intense panic, she couldn't help but repeat these questions over and over again: "Why and how could her salon be bad?" She would ask these questions while looking at me, but it was more like she was asking these questions to herself. This example shows that social devices of occultation, such as the use of therapeutic discourses by professional dominatrixes (Lindemann 2012) activated to protect oneself against the "whore stigma" (Pheterson 2001), are extremely effective but at the same time are tenuous. The competences not being formalized, the legitimacy of the practices initiated, and the reputation of the salon can be questioned easily. Once activated, the whore stigma can result in a destabilization of the psychic or somatic balance.

The terms "sadotherapist," "sex therapist," and "dominant therapist" can be interpreted in the light of Anne O'Nomis's analysis as the adaptation of an alter ego and a super self. But this obscures the difficulty of repressive laws, the isolation of dominatrixes, the fear of those who are assumed to be real whores, the stigmatization of those who have crossed boundaries with clients, and the stigmatization of BDSM sexualities in psychological discourses. The use of psychology as a definition of the self draws the contours of a self that tends to invisibilize the constraint that is expressed in the form of the labor market, the few opportunities that are available to a low-skilled migrant from a working-class background like Katerina and can then act as a false self. That being said, an interpretation of these personality traits in terms of a defense to push away the whore stigma is useful. This interpretation in the field of psychodynamics of work makes it possible to take into consideration this failure while allowing to reveal the positive aspects of the reference to the field of psychology. Indeed, it testifies to a desire to identify positively with a professional group composed of women, which is significant.

Notes

1

As Ronald Weitzer suggests: It is something of a misnomer to say that Germany "legalized" prostitution in 2002. It was legal before 2002, but German criminal law defined prostitution as immoral ("contrary to public decency and morality") and erotic businesses had a fuzzy, extra-legal, unregulated status. The 2002 law (ProstG) defined sex work as an occupation; gave workers the right to health care, social security, and unemployment benefits; and revised the offense of promoting prostitution (pimping) to apply only to individuals who infringe on a worker's "personal or financial independence".

(Weitzer 2017: 377)

2　Mistress Monique von Cleef was described as a sadotherapist for instance (see Monique von Cleef 1931).
3　This name was regularly used in medieval society from the 12th century onward to designate women in a relationship with a lover of lower social status than theirs, who adored and worshipped them and with whom they lived a chaste and pure love.

Bibliography

Bersani L. (1998). *Le rectum est-il une tombe?* Paris, EPEL.

Bidaud E. (2016). *Psychanalyse et pornographie*. Paris, La Musardine.

Boehringer S., Foucault M. (2015). Subjectivité et vérité. Cours au Collège de France. *Essaim*, 2(35), 159–162. Available on: http://www.cairn.info/revue-essaim-2015-2-page-159.htm. https://doi.org/10.3917/ess.035.0159

Butler J. (1990). *Gender Trouble: Feminism and the Subversion of Identity*. New Yok, Routledge.

von Cleef M. (1931). *The House of Pain. Secaucus. The Strange World of Mistress Monique von Cleef*. New Jersey, Lyle Stuart Inc./A Maurice Gerodias Book.

Dejours C. (2015) 1993. *Travail: Usure mentale*. Paris, Bayard.

Dejours C. (2018). 2001. *Le corps d'abord*. Paris, Payot.

Henry M. (1965). *Philosophie et phénoménologie du corps*. Paris, PUF.

Hochschild A. R. (1983). *The Managed Heart: Commercialization of Human Feeling*. Berkeley, University of California Press.

Levey T. G., Pinsky D. (2015a). 'A world turned upside down': Emotional labour and the professional dominatrix. *Sage Journal, Sexualities*, 18(4), 438–458.

Levey T. G., Pinsky, D. (2015b). A constellation of stigmas: intersectional stigma management and the professional dominatrix. *Deviant Behavior*, 36(5), 347–367.

Lindemann D (2011) 'Is that any way to treat a lady?': The dominatrix's dungeon. In C. Bobel and S. Kwan (Eds.), *Embodied Resistance: Challenging the Norms, Breaking the Rules*, 26–36. Nashville, TN, Vanderbilt University Press.

Lindemann D. (2012). *Dominatrix: Gender, Eroticism, and Control in the Dungeon*. Chicago, IL, University of Chicago Press.

Molinier P. (2000). Virilité défensive, masculinité créatrice. *Travail, genre et sociétés*, 3(1), 25–44.

Molinier P. (2006). *Les enjeux psychiques du travail*. Paris, Petite Bibliotheque Payot.

Molinier P. (2009). "Temps professionnel et temps personnel des travailleuses du *care*: perméabilité ou clivage?", *Temporalités* [En ligne], 9. mis en ligne le 30 septembre 2009, consulté le 02 avril 2022. http://journals.openedition.org/temporalites/988; https://doi.org/10.4000/temporalites.988

O'Connell Davidson J. (1998). *Prostitution, Power and Freedom*. Cambridge, Polity.

O'Neill M. (2001). *Prostitution and Feminism: Towards a Politics of Feeling*. Cambridge, Polity Press.

O'Nomis A. (2013). *The History and Arts of the Dominatrix*. Ebooks, Collector's edition ebook, Hafa Adai Books.

Parrenas R. S. (2012). Le travail de care des hôtesses de bar au Japon, *Revue internationale de psychopathologie et de psychodynamique du travail*, 2(28), 15–31, traduit de l'anglais par John Baker.

Pharo P. (1996). *L'injustice et le mal*. Paris, L'Harmattan.

Pheterson G. (2001). *Le prisme de la prostitution*. Paris, l'Harmattan, Bibliothèque du féminisme.

Rubin G. (1984) 1992. Thinking sex: Notes from a radical theory of the politics of sexuality. In C. S. Vance (Ed.), *Pleasure and Danger: Exploring Female Sexuality*, 267–319. London, Pandora Press.

Sanders T., O'Neill M., Pitcher J. (2009). *Prostitution: Sex Work, Policy and Politics*. London, Sage.

Weitzer R. (2017). Resistance to Sex Work Stigma, *Sexualities* (January 2017), DOI: 10.1177/1363460716684509

Movie

Polanski R. (2013). *La Vénus à la fourrure*, R. B. Production/A. S. Film, France.

3

THE IDEOLOGY OF FEMALE SUPREMACY IN THE NAME OF THE MOTHER

3.1 Introduction

Venus in Furs (Sacher–Masoch 2009) is a work that tells the story of the transformation of a love relationship into a freely consented slave contract. It has had a considerable influence in popular culture, in particular, by the practitioners of the female domination and quite especially by Female Supremacists (or Gynarchists).[1] But the influence of this novel in the academic world is also undeniable. In 1890, Richard von Krafft-Ebing, a psychiatrist, promoted masochism as a psychopathological category in *Psychopathia Sexualis* (Krafft-Ebing 1895), deriving it from the novel *Venus in Furs*. This work also served as a theoretical basis for the philosopher Gilles Deleuze in the study on masochism that he exposes in *Presentation of Sacher-Masoch: The Cold and the Cruel* (Deleuze 1967). According to him, Sacher-Masoch was inspired by Bachofen to subvert the patriarchy. Johann Jakob Bachofen was a Swiss historian and the author of *Das Mutterrecht* (Bachofen 1996), the most known synthesis of the big fresco of the matriarchal world. The matriarchy represents the stage of development that he calls the poetry of history, that is to say, a time of justice and peace, fraternity and equality, where everyone is united in the name of the maternal principle. In his view, women, in spite of their physical inferiority, impose themselves in the first phases of the development of humanity because they control the religious rites. With Deleuze, one can think that Sacher-Masoch was himself inspired by his contemporary Bachofen to dream the Venus because "[t]he fantasy finds here what it needs, a theoretical, ideological structure, which gives it the value of a general conception of human nature and the world" (Deleuze 1967: 47). If we go along with Gilles Deleuze's hypothesis, it is then not surprising that gynarchists refer with such enthusiasm to *Venus in Furs* and that Bachofen's theses on matriarchy have also greatly influenced Female Supremacists' works. Gynarchists' essays

DOI: 10.4324/9781003258537-5

are intended to propagate the idea that at the origin of humanity, there is something divine in women, that "female authority instituted by nature has caused
the male to submit to the female and thus proclaim the superiority of the female
sex" (d'Arbrant 1997). In these essays, the sexuality of men is used by women to
put them at their service and to make them obedient. They describe a fiction of
history where the male gender would have usurped the power naturally devolved
to women. This would explain why the world would be in full degeneration. In
this utopia, certain parts of history and mythologies are reinterpreted in order
to legitimize this political system. Thus, cooperation serves defensive processes
through the construction of a "defensive ideology."

I discovered this subculture with Lèchebotte with whom I continued an epistolary relationship for about a year. I realized that his "beautiful speeches" were
not addressed to me but directed toward the internal object of a fantasy, similar
to that of the muse. It is, The imaginary loss that obsesses so much the melan-
cholic proposal of the Female Supremacists does not concern any real object. It
is the impossible capture of fantasy that her strategy aims at. The fantasy belongs
to an order of meaning prior to the order of experience (Laplanche and Pontalis
1998). Thus, by playing the unreal loss against the real event, the gynarchist
writings in the prism of melancholy subtract women from their history, their
subjectivity, and their words.

The paradoxical relation to the real, which is thus outlined, must be questioned. This chapter will be the object of an analysis of the processes generated
in the relationship between the production of fantasies and the social link that we
weave with others. The interviews with gynarchists who evoke their amorous
adventures put in evidence "the 'ambiguous trade' of the melancholy" (Agamben
1998: 57), which is the index of a certain relation to the other where a specific
form of subjectivation is played. It is about a subjectivation that includes the
possibility of an emancipation in relation to this alienation chosen by the subject
himself but means also numerous pitfalls (Popa 2014: 153). The profile of the
masochist in this novel, as Deleuze had already noted, is that of "a victim who
seeks an executioner, and who needs to train him, to persuade him, and to make
an alliance with him for the strangest enterprise" (Deleuze 1967: 14). This can
lead to a gradual tolerance by women for an organization of the script that goes
against their desire, their needs, and even their health. The exceeding of limits or
their non-recognition in those contexts could be related to "a rigid script" which
leads to "misunderstand[ing] the partner's signals" (Wetzstein et al. 1993). The
question of "subjective moral autonomy" (Dejours 2015 [1993]) then arises, that
is to say, of the subject's capacity to resist the collective ideal when it leads to the
worst: threatening, excluding, and betraying one's word. A taking of distance
and of autonomy with regard to the capture by the idealization of the object must
be accomplished.

Taking social life as an object of reflection highlights the material conditions of existence that have made sexual masochism possible in this form. This
gives the opportunity to reveal the mobilized gendered defenses (virility and

muliebrity) that prevent the perception of injustice and the conditions that make it possible. I will therefore begin to restore these current theories where the masochism of men would be at the service of the restoration of the natural power of the mother until then suspended outside of time and history within the framework of their current communities.

3.2 Female Supremacists as communities?

3.2.1 S/M vs. Female Supremacy

Despite many similarities, there are dividing lines that separate gynarchists from the totality of sadomasochists. These are not just organizational subdivisions: the gynarchist and BDSM orientation separates two major subcultural areas from each other, whose independence is very pronounced in many ways. Even if the collective forms of organization, the practices, many fetish elements, the language, and, in principle, also the mode of subcultural structuring are identical, gynarchy is a real subculture on its own that spreads through drawings like Sardax, who is one of the most established contemporary artists in the Female Supremacy genre. Many books on the subjects also exist with recognized authors who have bestsellers to their credit as *No Escape from Matria* (Ritter 2021), *The Training Farm: A Journey into Submission* (Harris 2015), and *Finding Love through Female Domination* (Lane 2016).

On the Internet, periodical online articles and promotional and training materials can easily be found on YouTube channels, for instance, from the Female Supremacy University[2] or Gynarchyrule;[3] in a broader sense, it is possible to become a member of discussion groups and take part in munch and other events dedicated to Female Supremacy.

Female Supremacists combine an interest in female domination with particular ideas of female worship, special rituals, and a worldview in which women have absolute power over men, as developed by the S/M church community in the Bay Area in the 1970s (Scott 1997: 124). Women and men who call themselves Supremacists or gynarchists assert that women are superior to men by blending the concepts of feminism, matriarchy, and belief in a supreme goddess. In this type of deification, there is indeed an idealization and an ideal of the self[4] in the service of the gynarchy. Here, cohesion is fueled by an imaginary collusion and the election of a common enemy – men whom women should educate and enslave using sexuality to force them into slaves. Freud's formula, to express sexual difference, made women the beloved and men the lovers (Freud 1924). These authors reverse the formula so that the torturer is the lover and the new castrated man loves her. "In this inversion nothing changes except for the psychic identifications that are still welded for the production of difference married with the facticity of anatomically correct bodies." As revolutionary as they claim to be, "[i]t is still a woman who must save the world by saving men from themselves" (Hart 2003: 133).

The specificity of Female Supremacy is manifested in certain stylistic features that are represented in the media whose main function seems to be the stimulation of the imagination, the sexual stimulation. These representations denote a certain preference for educational authority relations, for example, by representing a school example of corporal punishment. Jay Em specializes in scenes of domestic discipline, and the majority of his pictures feature women beating severely their masculine partners in a moralistic way,[5] and the arrangement of styles like the equestrian style for women or particularities such as the incorporation of certain motifs of a historical character such as Greco-Roman or ahistorical scenes borrowing them from the mythical character of the Amazons as the drawing of Sardax, *Sentiments from an Enslaved Sissy*. In this respect, gynarchist women on the net often take names of goddesses as "Goddess Kali," "Goddess Kaila," or "Goddess Aphrodite." Female Supremacists' behavior often involves a strong emphasis on magical realm, a furry queen perhaps with a chariot pulled by her devoted admirers naked in chains like slaves, a predilection for certain sexual practices such as special ligature games, forced feminization, miniaturization of men, ponyboy training, forniphilia, or even special anal manipulations such as insertion of artificial limbs and cunnilingus that one can largely find in *The Art of Sardax* (Sardax 2006).

An important phenomenon is the mediating role of their ideological superstructure in mediating certain attitudes and demarcation from the outside. Thus, in the Female Supremacists theme, the idea of the scarcity of real believers in gynarchy, passionate, and authentic plays a particular role. I received a number of messages along these lines, from Female Supremacists like John, whom I met on *FetLife*, writing me that he wishes there were more believers in Australia on *FetLife*. This regret indicating nostalgia, longing for something better, is part of the affirmation of gynarchist identity. The identification with the group of belonging is translated from the interior by the prevalence of a gynarchist spirit directed toward the veneration of the female body. It is then possible to lean on the group through an identification with this one, an adhesion to its ideology. The signs of belonging to the ideology have a lot to do with a number of rituals that mark the separation. In this regard, The S/M Church in San Francisco, The Femina Society, The Church of Jesus the Flagellant, and The Gynarchic Order of the East are gynarchist organizations that offer religious or spiritual services dedicated to the worship of the goddess and rituals instituted to enable the submissive to attain divine perfections. In BDSM communities, as within the gynarchist universe, the prosecution of those rituals that make possible the subculture identification is closely related to a "symbol of purification." That's in order to reinforce this symbol that in "the S/M church in San Francisco, those who take communion must kneel down and be hit on the shoulders and head" (d'Arbrant 1997: 40).

The function of representation, mediated by images and drawings of gynarchist women wearing certain clothes, plays in itself a role of call to order. In the representations of the flogging scene, for example, the men are naked to make the blows perceptible, while the gynarchists' clothing of riding pants and fur hides the bodies of the gynarchist women. These representations abound on the Internet, up to apparently fictional descriptions of the experiences of apprentice slaves where the attention is focused on the ornaments and clothes of the women and the bruised body of the slaves. It is evident in all the illustrations of Nanshakh as in the representation of *Gynarchistan, the country of full employment* (Nanshakh 2022).[6]

Certain practices and narratives support the gynarchist ideology. I am thinking in particular of the representation of women in these images where they seem to have no interest in seeking erotic sensations. In Nadine's adventure, for example, women are represented as pure, innocent, and serving order and virtue over their own slaves and in their couples with the primary intention of founding a gynarchist society (d'Arbrant 1997). Gynarchist ideas about the education of the slave play a role in this attitude.

Then, the entry in the community here cannot be summarized as an attraction for D/S relationships. It also induces the adhesion to an ideal, values, a society, and an adhesion that involves the whole person. In this regard, the demarcation with sadomasochistic groups is a crucial content referring to this defensive ideology. Gynarchists consider themselves freer and more emancipated to sadomasochists. For Henry, a gynarchist, submissive sadomasochist men are described as often disrespectful, trapped in thought by pornographic representations. Mistress Katherine, a gynarchist, thinks that sadomasochistic sexuality is a prisoner of the ideology of male domination.

3.2.2 A fantasy that remains in the shadow of melancholy

The vision of sexuality given by the gynarchists is questioned by the members of the BDSM community, or at least it is discussed. This vision of BDSM is far from being unanimous. For many submissives and dominatrixes, BDSM practices are generally realized within a session, a game, or even a play, which, in turn, is realized within a determinable time frame and boundaries. BDSM thus implies a playful character. But since Female Supremacists prefer speaking about a lifestyle rather than a game, there is no distinction that can be made between what is a play and what is not a play. Specifically, there are elements of violence that appear in some gynarchist practices such as castration practices that make the distinction between play and power relations problematic.

Mistress Cassandra, a 41-year-old French venal dominatrix, whom I met during the Master's research in 2010, finds this form of 24 hours' sexuality aberrant. According to her experience, people who have entered their role permanently have lost their footing with reality. Female Supremacy is a utopia because S/M is above all a game! According to her, this type of relationship doesn't make sense because it is not reconcilable with a family life, work relations, and generally speaking, a social life. The gynarchized man would have no life at all and would live all his life through S/M, which would denote a psychological health problem.

> For the domina this sort of 24 hours relationship, it is to have a ball and chain hanging on the foot, or a "big child" to whom you have to tell everything: most of the time, the submissive is stuck to the words of his mistress like a mussel to the rock, without taking any initiative.

Many participants like Stefane consider that gynarchists would only live their fantasy in their head without ever facing the reality. We can argue that the difficulty of the participants to confront their expectations with the reality meets obstacles. Many objective difficulties stand in the way of fulfilling gynarchist desires in relationships. The relatively small number of like-minded people makes it impossible for isolated gynarchists to find others. That's why Mistress Sandra, like so many other members living in the provinces, travels to larger cities or abroad. As she mentions, "[S]ocial networks like *Fetlife* make contact possible even over great distances." However, the specificity of the gynarchist interest, in particular the restriction to a sadomasochistic role, active or passive, and the political justifications that accompany it, leads to a reduction in the chances of finding a partner. For some of the people involved, only a few people qualify as partners, and geographical distances hinder many people from making the first move. The search for a partner with openly gynarchist desires can remain fruitless for a lifetime, often stops at a few individual experiences, and leads to resignation for many.

That being said, gynarchists constitute a specific form of practitioners where the writing of fantasies plays a particularly important role. If the main function of BDSM communities, from the point of view of those involved, is to make sadomasochistic desires realizable, the fantasists (*fantasmateurs*) constitute a specific form of practitioners who focus mainly on writing their fantasies and put off any opportunity for carnal encounters as much as possible. The *fantasmateurs* are the names given in general to men who are not able to pass to the real. This, already described by Krafft-Ebing (1895),[7] is nothing new. On the contrary, in his eyes sexual practice appears only as an episode in the sexual life of the pervert, which is dominated by fantasy and imagination. It is not surprising to find many *fantasmateurs* among the gynarchists, given the impressive fantasies by the radicalness of the consequences that their implementation would mean. I particularly remember a man with whom I had an appointment, in his thirties, quite introverted in his attire but quite open about his fantasies. He invited me to a restaurant; spoke to me about his different experiences with dominant slavic women, with whom he acted as a stooge, driver, or houseworker; and then spoke to me about his castration fantasy. I needed him to clarify and asked if it was not a question of real castration. He told me that if the woman was really dominant (as in his fantasy), he would do it and then spend the rest of his life serving as a slave to dominant women. So if he didn't do it, it's simply that he didn't meet a woman who was dominant enough. This is what we call, in BDSM parlance, the prototypical *fantasmateur*. After having given me those confidences, he feels strangely uncomfortable all of a sudden. He tells me that he wants to go and get some cigarettes, which he left in his car. I waited 15 minutes, 20 minutes, and then I understood that he would not come back. He called me back 3 months later. He shakes, he says he wants to see me again, and I finally recognize his voice. I am dumbfounded. He embarrassedly told me that he had been struck by my "dominance" and had no choice but to run away. Other gynarchists like Benoit regularly publish his fantasies that he takes for realities. I started corresponding with Benoit because I was touched by his story that I had read on a website. He had written to me about his relationship with his wife, where progressively she would have made him put a leash on her and then made him eat next to her instead of the dog. I noticed while visiting other sites on female domination that he had posted several of these messages and that he contradicted himself from one discussion to the next. In one message he said he was happy in his relationship, while in another discussion group he complained about women who "only wanted his money," a typical complaint of a submissive and dissatisfied suitor as I explained in Chapter 1. This attitude can be interpreted as a defense strategy to avoid having to admit that he was afraid of confronting the real world. But what "fantasy gains us in terms of compensation and instantaneous coherence pays off in terms of a fair understanding of the larger meaning of what is experienced" (Popa 2014: 154). Indeed, in his struggle to make reality match what he expects, he works against the women who run the risk of thwarting his desire for female sexuality and surprising him by stigmatizing them as whores. In doing so, he also works against himself, moving further and further away from the terrain of his lived experience, preferring the weightlessness of an imaginary world clouded by the taboo of homosexuality where any test of contrariness is carefully avoided.

3.2.3 The notion of subculture questioned through the lens of psychodynamic of work

Can we speak of a community of gynarchists? Even if people are engaged in discussion groups, meeting spaces, and media with the intention of meeting a person with whom to realize his fantasies or simply to stimulate desire, sexual stimulation is not enough to ensure the collective function because, as Dejours mentions,

> love alone can't act as a factor of culture, in the sense of a reversal of egoism into altruism. It is thus necessary to underline the centrality of normative agreements: norms, rules, values, ethical springs of living together. In the principle of organized human groups, it is indeed the requirement of cooperation, the will to work together, to make common work which mobilizes the formation of links between individuals, and not the libido.
>
> *(Dejours 2009)*

The collective function is provided in the belief in a societal ideal and the desire to create an indirect or direct bond with like-minded people, the emergence of a sometimes combative self-consciousness, and the acceptance of oneself as a mistress or a slave. Then the importance of this function can be seen in the search for validation by peers and the doubts of isolated and insecure sadomasochists who seek advice, for example, in the many letters they write in blogs dedicated to gynarchy like *suprematiefeminine-o2.erog* that constantly offer advice, models, help, and enlightenment. The range of possibilities for mutual support, protection, and guidance extends from the initiation of inexperienced people to gynarchist rules and philosophy/education of the gynarchist's slave and educational advice for the gynarchist mistress to legal advice in case of concrete problems.

That being said, the few elements of investigation gathered suggest that Female Supremacy covers in reality a constellation of sites, blogs, and discussion groups that have little in common. The observations of the field show that some people who created Female Supremacist groups aren't genuinely interested or invested in the creation of a gynarchist society. Supporting evidence: people who created gynarchist sites while not identifying themselves with the gynarchy. Then, the recognition is played in the illusion. In a mail I wrote in 2016 to the moderator of a site dedicated to gynarchy, she admitted that she plays on the principle of gynarchy because she notices a demand on the male side about those fantasies, but she herself didn't take the concept that seriously, because it's a kind of fascism that induces the superiority of one sex over the other. Another man I spoke with in 2015, who runs a blog where he posts gynarchic columns, admitted that he didn't consider himself as gynarchist. "The idea that women are inherently superior to men is just as absurd as the reverse. It's just a fantasy really. I simply wrote about a future society Gynarchic to reconcile three passions: Female Domination, writing and science fiction."

In the same ways, the interviews I conducted with gynarchists can make us doubt about a culture based on common values for the Female Supremacists. For instance, gynarchy is sometimes confused with Female-Led Relationships (FLRs). It is the case in the article "Long Live Gynarchy: Beginning of an FLR."[8] In FLR, the dynamic of the relationship lies also in the fact that the woman takes the initiative within the couple and assumes the position of dominant partner. However, couples like Steve and Suzanne have chosen this type of relationship by mutual agreement, considering it in terms of preference and not in political and ideological terms as is the case in a gynarchic setting. As Renee Lane (2016) mentions, gynarchy is about taking power over men. You don't ask them for their opinion!

This confusion in the understanding of gynarchy makes us ask the question of cultural heritage. It is indeed the cultural inheritance that ensures the continuity of the existence and that is an extension of the potential space between the subject and his environment. The culture, in the sense of Donald Winnicott (1975), refers to the tradition from which one inherits. It is something that is the common lot of humanity to which individuals and groups can contribute, and from which everyone will be able to draw something, if we have a place to put what we find. This place is a space where we try to share something with others in the hope of being understood. It is a space between me and my environment, a potential place of contribution to cultural experience transcending personal experience. The investment of this place is a condition of creation and individuation. The absence of agreement on common values and heritage can prevent the awareness of a community spirit, and it can also hinder people by isolating them. It has an impact on physical and psychological vulnerability by leading people, for example, to remain in toxic relationships.

3.3 Lèchebotte: an enchanted meeting under the sign of courtly love

I met Lèchebottes (Licking Boots) through Facebook at the beginning of my investigation on the net. He introduced himself to me as a married man, looking for dominant friends to play with his wife. Lèchebotte started to exchange in a formal way by showing extreme politeness and even extreme servility toward me as toward all women. He tells me that I am a dominant woman; "a raw pearl," he says. With Lèchebottes, I quickly get the impression that he is lecturing me in order to educate me to become a perfect sadist "and make an alliance with him to set up a strange enterprise," like the masochist described by Deleuze in *Le froid et le cruel* (Deleuze 1967: 14). As a testament to this, one time when I apologized, he told me, "never apologize!" as if to make me realize my rights over men and to "put me in my place" as a dominant, which was an order he gave himself. I never met Lèchebottes in person. Our letter-writing relationship lasted at least a year.

Lèchebotte is not just using polite phrases in a stereotypical way, as we will see many submissives do online. He is fluent in the French language. He works for diplomacy, and the use of a sustained French is thus in continuity with this same administrative work as well as the formulas of use: madam, miss, and politeness, which he uses abundantly. Here is an extract from a letter he sent me:

> Mrs. Gabrielle,
>
> You entrusted me with a duty, that of giving you an account, a description of what I thought of you and of our conversation a short while ago.
>
> I willingly bend to your will, in this matter as in all others, since docility is in my nature (as you so well pointed out).
>
> First of all, I am very happy that you have agreed to finally call me "Lèchebotte," as I asked you to do, and perhaps you will call me by my first name regularly. This indicates a progression in our relationship that I sincerely welcome. I like to think that you are gradually getting the taste (or at least the habit) of knowing that I am (virtually) at your beck and call, ready to answer all your questions obediently. I hope you will make use of this position of authority which is yours. It is quite clear that I am not asking for anything because I have nothing concrete to offer immediately, I am not trying to seduce you, to convince you of this or that, or other things of this kind, but I appreciate your conversation and I find it enriching.

For many submissives, like the *fantasmateur*, the writing of such erotic messages experienced through the lens of masochism is already part of the realization of their desire. Here the art of mastering poetry, politeness, and good manners and addressing me as an unattainable raw pearl is not without reminding the form of love lived in the courtly love. Courtly love in the Middle Ages is a conception of love based on desire and the notion of courtesy, referring to a set of values and manners found particularly in the milieu of the nobility. As Jacques Lacan reminds us in *The Ethics of Psychoanalysis*, courtly love

> is the creation of a circle of scholars. The first of them, William of Poitiers, lived between 1071 and 1126, his granddaughter Eleanor of Aquitaine and her daughter, Mary of Champagne, contributed to the dissemination of the precepts and rules of love as codified in 1186 by André Le Chapelain.
>
> *(Lacan 1986: 133)*

They also animated courts of love where judgments were pronounced in reference to the laws of love. The *fin'amor* is an idealized love for the Lady, married, often of a superior and inaccessible condition. The platonic relationship between the lover and his Lady was modeled on the medieval relationship between vassal and suzerain. The man is at the service of his Lady, with the monitoring of her desires, and must devote to her a fidelity without limits. The reference to courtly love in the case of Lèchebottes is particularly suitable. Indeed, the stories that he publishes use images of recurrent references in a medieval historical fantasy reality that determine the construction of her fantasy. The staging of a medieval world refers to an inaccessible, haughty chatelaine, the interior of a house to an aristocrat comfortably installed in her living room; for example, a stable will feature a horsewoman with a noble, haughty appearance like the story of Tiz he published on his Facebook Wall.

> Tiz would get up around 7:00 am every morning and arrives at the stables around 7:30 am in her riding clothes (high black leather dressage boots hand sewn to size, riding breeches usually in sand or buff color and a Barbour hunting jacket). She would first inspect the horses to see if everything was okay (the horses in her stables were fed around 6:00 am, by professional grooms who left once their task was done). Then she would go up to the basement above the tack room, to the small apartment that served as both my bedroom and my mistress's play area, which was the entire length of the building and had a high wooden frame. The room was the whole length of the building and the wooden frame was high, so there was plenty of room to wave the long whip that my mistress loved to use on me. Every morning Tiz would wake me up with a big whip across my buttocks. I was startled by an electric shock. With this method, no difficulty waking up, you are immediately up. Tiz had taught me good manners and I had to throw myself at her feet and kiss her boots. She would take a chair and I would start

licking the dust and other small dirt that had stuck to the leather when she was in the horses' boxes. Meanwhile, she would enjoy her first cigarette of the day with a cup of coffee (she brought her little Thermos from the kitchen in the main house). During my training, she had developed the habit of throwing the ashes of her cigarettes into my mouth; it had become an established tradition and this morning's episode was no exception.

Lèchebottes

These fantasies answer a desire to celebrate a distant past fantasized. It signals by indirection the presence of the consumer society of the beginning of the year 1970 with the Thermos, for example. It is tinged with a nostalgia of the horse civilization which marked the Western history in the Middle Ages. It restores, at the same time, the fundamentally medieval spirit: the duality of the medieval man, divided between an earthly impulse toward the scatological and a spiritual elevation toward the eschatological, in particular in the importance granted to his education or training. One can recall Jacques Le Goff that "it is the fact of the Middle Ages to always put in front the very high and the very low," which is revealing of a tendency to blur the demarcation between sacred and profane, between "holy day" and "holiday" (Bisson 1999: 245).

The analysis of the fantasies of Lèchebottes constructed through the lens of the codes and social imaginary of courtly love shows us that fantasies are always experienced within the cultural framework from which they emerge. In this, there is never anything like pure fantasy, and it has already been formed by the cultural history and experience of each individual, regardless of his or her material condition and existence.

As Louis-Georges Tin (2008) shows, courtesy in the Middle Ages was a lure. In fact, courtly love is rooted in the discourse of fealty, of fidelity to the person, that served the causes of the feudal power. By drawing attention to the things that remain within the official discourse of deference, the soldiers can lower the risk involved in courting women of higher rank. The mystification of love not only serves to disguise their sexual purpose but also provides a retreat that can soften the consequences of eventual discovery. The mystification of courtly love by soldiers, bachelors, and all the others also serves to reinforce royal control. They were domesticated, calmed down, and polished by distilling the favors of the lady: a look, an attention, a delicacy perhaps, but nothing more. Thus maintained in the dependence of the lady, and thus of the suzerain, they reinforced the feudal power (Tin 2008).

One may wonder if it is the same for today's dominas (this name was regularly used in medieval society from the 12th century onward to designate women in a relationship with a lover of lower social status than their own, with whom they lived a chaste and pure love). As a matter of fact, the writing of the fantasies of Lèchebottes and the beautiful speeches that he wrote are not really addressed to me but oriented toward the internal object of his fantasies. This autobiography makes us aware of the paradox at the heart of the analysis of masochism experienced in his way. Like the masochistic partner in *Venus in Furs*, Lèchebottes envisioned me as a woman who lacked nothing, which was divorced from my experience as a woman living in economic hardship at the time. This division between theory and experience, the subject and the object, and the private and the public is, for Teresa de Lauretis, a semiotician, the paradox of the woman:

> The paradox of the being that is simultaneously prisoner and absent from the discourse, it is constantly talked about but it is itself inaudible or unspeakable, shown as spectacle and still not represented or not representable, invisible, yet constituted as object and guarantee of the vision; a being whose existence and specificity are simultaneous.
>
> *(de Lauretis 1990: 115)*

3.4 The role of sublimation in the fantasies of Lèchebottes

In the November 23, 1960 session of the seminar *Le Transfert dans sa disparité subjective*, Lacan evokes courtly love to say that it is not the same thing as Greek love, but that "it occupies an analogous function in society. I mean that it is obviously of the order and function of sublimation" (Lacan 1960: 25). In fact, courtly love gives a form to the impossibility of sexual intercourse.

> Thus, the cause of desire is displaced "in" the Lady, who becomes that to which access calls for the mediation of a space of play intended to guarantee the margin indispensable to the indefinite relaunch of desire. The lover must then pass through the spurt of poetic discovery – through the trobar – to enjoy the Lady.
>
> *(Vivès 2011: 18)*

As in courtly love, the women portrayed in these male fantasies are almost always women of higher rank. This gap between social statuses makes the woman inaccessible and elevates her to the rank of gods to be adored. It is a woman endowed with exceptional beauty and merits, who is married, accomplished. The "class," the "elegance," the "arrogance," and the natural "authority" of the dominant woman of which he speaks to me function at the same time as factors of integration, attesting to the membership of a class, as well as a factor of exclusion, allowing to distinguish oneself from the "inferior" classes. In this conception, arrogance tends to expel the other to mark the limits of identity.

Lèchebottes, just like *L'amant courtois*, is totally submissive and devoted to his lady: abnegation, obedience, and discretion are his watchwords. To deserve the love of his lady (who is cold and capricious), in order to prove the intensity and constancy of his love, he bends to her services in the expectation of emerging victorious from a series of tests often set by his mistress – a strong notion of servitude and also of self-sacrifice, which are particularly striking in the fantasies of Lèchebottes:

> When my rupture with my beautiful English Woman was consummated (she dismissed me with a bang when I announced to her that I could not abandon my studies to follow her abroad), I was drowned in a very great sadness. I cursed myself for my cowardice. I had not been worthy of her and her demands. I had passed up the opportunity to become her slave for life, precisely because I had been afraid, selfishly, to be only her slave and nothing more.

As in the institution of courtly love, the partners of Lèchebottes do not love him. At least, he doesn't know it, and he was never so sure of existing in the eyes of the Other as when he suffers. He "does not hope for the love of the women, at most [he] hope[s] for their pity, their recognition." If he prefers, however, to remain in relationships where he is dissatisfied, or not loved in return, it is that they allow him to sublimate as in the *fin'amor*. Courtly love embodies, in the field of sublimation, a purified desire. Lacan advances, "A quite refined way of making up for the absence of sexual intercourse, by pretending that it is we who put an obstacle in its way" (Lacan 1972–1973: 65). In short, the chastity exalted rests on the rejection of pleasure. A gap is then forever dug between the demand (i.e. the service of goods) and the desire. In fact, behaving like the knight in the Middle Ages who suffers everything for his lady, being satisfied with what she wants to offer him, with small attention, with "little things," it is also what he prefers since it boosts his desire.

While Lèchebotte didn't seem to have problems with women's inferiority, he didn't like being thought of as "a real guy," being perceived as inferior to sexually dominant men. The dominant men irritate him deeply. For him, there is no such thing as a dominant man; it is an aberration; women are superior, more intelligent, and more beautiful than men; and men are basically dependent on the goodwill of these ladies in terms of desire. One finds in him the same "aura" of naturalness that surrounds his fantasies. When I write to him that I have masochistic fantasies too, he doesn't approve of a "woman of my standing" giving herself to low-quality guys who don't realize the superiority of women. His rhetoric is so well worked that I come to think that if the woman affirms her desires toward other men, her loves and her phallic jouissance, his whole fantasy world is in danger. Some women that Lèchebotte was in contact with and to whom he submitted himself had confided to him that in life, "they needed a guy, a real guy." These words I heard myself many times from dominant women who could not imagine themselves with submissive men in concubinage as Maîtresse Divina, a Parisian dominatrix that I had interviewed in 2018. I wanted to have his opinion on this. He would defend himself by writing back, "You have to have balls to let them be crushed by women in heels." He behaved toward women for whom he expressed his desire in a very demonstrative, and thus one could even say, in an essentially virile way. He reported to me, offended, that a dominant man had written to him, the latter being in search of a boot-licker to shine his shoes. He had made a point of telling me that he only served women. These remarks resonate with Lacan's idea of sublimation: "The idea that sublimation is this effort to allow love to be realized with the woman, and not only to pretend that it happens with the woman." One can then make the hypothesis that the inflation of women's love by men in the line of courtly love is a consequence of the social relation between the sexes. It is intrinsically linked to the guilt implanted (in the sense of Foucault) in the subjectivity of men to counter their desire. If anal sex is part of these fantasies, as I can deduce based on the practices described in many of them, it is surrounded by a decorum that makes this practice "acceptable." One can understand that he is not able to affirm his desire of penetration in front of the power because of the taboo of homosexuality associated and that he must disguise it under the features of an idealized love for the women. Indeed, the gynarchist ideal of Lèchebottes remains first of all a heterosexual affair lived through the lens of the escape of a homosexual choice. That is what one can conclude through the reading of some of the fantasies of Lèchebotte's for example, the following cuckolding gynarchist fantasy questions the binary opposition between homosexuality and heterosexuality by allowing the author of the fantasy to be a spectator and to take pleasure by putting himself in the place of all the actors and actresses of the scene:

> Leila helped me then greatly, in her way .... At the time she lived two steps from my house and she immediately proposed to take me in her car. Of course, she gained superbly from it: I was in full lack and I transferred all my submission drives towards her. She was treated like a princess of royal blood. The leather of her boots was polished to a mirror finish, her riding gear was carefully maintained. When she arrived at the arena, she would go straight to the clubhouse for coffee while I prepared and saddled her horse: she never had to bend down or do anything strenuous in the arena (not even light her cigarette, I would see to that when I was near her and she reached for her pack of cigarettes). She loved to give me futile and absurd orders to see how I would react. She was like a child testing her new toy. She especially liked it when I licked her boots (in private, not in front of the other riders. She liked to tell me that she was a fulfilled woman because she had a lover to lick her sex and a slave to lick her boots. ... She later met the man who eventually became her husband and through whom she gained financial independence and a prospect of a stable and prosperous marriage (something I could not hope to give her given my own situation). There was a brief period of overlapping where the two suitors vied with each other in gifts and attention to capture the attention of the beautiful one, whose boots I assiduously licked three or four times a week. As a good Mediterranean woman, she despised me for my submission, I was not manly enough for her taste (I also had the defect of being a student, of having no situation, no comfort to offer her). If I didn't interest her as a man, I was at least convenient and practical as a slave.

For Lèchebottes, the idealization of love is a condition sine qua non of the public expression of the desire of being penetrated. It allows, by attributing to women divine qualities, to nourish its pretension to dictate its way of doing in a ritual way. If, on the one hand, the idealization of love confirms the way dominant men want to be perceived, it allows Lèchebottes to express his desires of this form of sexuality in a culture where their expressions are taboo for men. This is where he is in his relationship with Leila: since he cannot be her submissive wife and she his object, he creates the idealized relationship to what is deemed insufficient in him, what has been rejected. Let us not forget, as Lacan recalls in *Le séminaire l'angoisse,* that "his culture has made him cease, he has let go of the culture of his narcissism, his self care, her coquetry, his beauty, in order to become knight servant of the lady" (Lacan 1967).

These cultural fantasies constitute the framework of personal fantasies. Given their intrinsic link to guilt, it can be difficult to dislodge them, to displace them, and to create between them and oneself the distance from which it becomes possible to assume what one is, at the crossroads of personal history and his culture. Faced with these contradictions, its conflicts lead some men gynarchists, as it was in the case of Lèchebottes, to disappear from one day to the next, taking the decision to flee the relationship without warning.

3.5 The dangers of practices lived under the prism of fantasies where the mother is idealized

In courtly love, as in gynarchy, the submissives seem to praise the same person. In this context, one may wonder about the relationship between the production of gynarchists' fantasies and the social bond established with gynarchist women. We can argue that in the context of gynarchist relationships, participants' relationships with their fantasies are particularly ambiguous because of the "rule of exchange" that gynarchist relationships attempt to relive in the flesh. They try to correspond a lifestyle to adopt 24 hours, a rule of social game through the masochistic contract, sealing formally the agreement of two subjectivities. So the transition between fantasy and reality is difficult, no time and no space being thought about to gradually disengage from the other's hold. This is what differentiates gynarchic relationships from BDSM relationships. The social practices within the BDSM scene and the theme of cruelty are only linked within the notion of play. The practiced violence has a fixed frame, which can be interrupted at any time and which distinguishes it, for example, from the violence or cruelty of a torture (Deremetz 2018: 95). Sandra, a gynarchist who spends a lot of time in this role of queen, highlights the risk of being cut off from the real world that a gynarchist type of relationship involves.

> I like to live the gynarchy. I'm careful because the problem is that when you live like that, you decide everything, you are the queen. At the beginning it was complicated in my private life with my friends, sometimes

I gave orders, I gave my suitcase to be pulled, and I didn't understand why they don't take my bag or open the door for me; sometimes I felt a little bit down to earth. Now I try to find a balance so that I don't let myself be carried away because sometimes I've seen myself waiting for my things to be taken away.

In this relation to the other, role-playing loses its role of distancing the participants from reality. This may cause concern among the participants and spectators of the BDSM scene: is it real or a theatrical performance? Henry's interview shows that within gynarchist relationships, insofar as the notion of play does not exist, it seems way more difficult to determine what constitutes play, which can lead to power abuse:

> There was abuse of power with my first owner. She was not very stable psychologically. She lied a lot and did some very dishonest things. She used cannabis and she was a liar, she lied about her past, about her work, about her diplomas, about everything. So I can say that there was abuse of trust more than abuse of power, I wanted to separate and run away, but she always managed to manipulate me. By sex mainly, and seduction, and intimidation, and using my commitment. It's easier when you are submissive. She could also threaten to divulge the nature of our relationship while I worked in the military. I rationalized it because at the time it was very rare to have a gynarchist relationship. The fact that I was in a 24/7 relationship meant that very quickly I found myself following the protocol to serve obediently and forgot a little about the other problems that she had posed. I am naturally submissive to women, so it is easier for a woman to manipulate me. **All is not erotic permanently, but the gynarchist relation allows to eroticize everything**.

One sees here that following the protocol is a way of neutralizing thought and reducing the capacity for distancing, for standing back, and for reflexivity. Activism is also mobilized to narrow the space necessary for the play of subjectivity particularly in anxiety-provoking situations. He also rationalized "because at the time it was very rare to be able to live a gynarchist relation." The paradox is as follows: protocol that should allow practices to be carried out in a safe, healthy, and consensual framework is mobilized to carry out practices in a preferentially operative mode in a state of alert to avoid thinking.

In these gynarchist relationships, the question of the subjective moral autonomy[9] arises then, that is to say, of the capacity of the subject to resist the collective ideals of gynarchy when this one leads to lie, to betray its word, and to manipulate. Indeed, the intelligence used only to the service of the abstractions of the theory involves the risk of loss of relation to the world, and it participates in cruelty. Among numerous pitfalls, Sonia's relationship with gynarchy highlights that those relationships could involve the possibility of an alienation when the absence of sexual fantasy prevents the emergence of human desire, and the opening into an authentic relationship.

The ideal gynarchist incarnated in the representations of indifferent, cold, and pure women painted as goddesses who would get what they want from men, born of the cleavage of the phallic object, has pushed some women like her to invest themselves in gynarchy without having sexual fantasies related to this form of sexuality. I asked Sonia what she liked about gynarchy. She answered that it was the control of the submissive's sexuality, but she referred to a phase where she was severely depressed and her "libido was more and more descending" and where she thinks she cannot satisfy a man sexually. So all the practices that she imagines to be parts of the gynarchic decorum – the confinement, the chastity cage, the obligation for the submissive not to see his domina when he makes love, therefore for her, the possibility of hiding her body – please her very much, in the sense that it suits her and reassures her. Sonia gives here elements that accredit the image of the dominant woman who does not express any desire. The dominant woman assumes frigidity as a modality of her seduction. What pleases her is the possibility the domination offers, to never show her body, and in spite of that to have a man at her feet who takes care of her, distraught with love. Her attraction to gynarchy is combined with the fantasy of a man who would also be the bearer of the values of care, thus appealing to a form of reciprocity in the concern (of desire) of the other. Thus, the agreed discourse on the control of the submissive's sexuality quickly gives way to another more authentically invested aspect that concerns the possibility of living a relationship while avoiding intimacy and sexuality. For Sonia, the heterosexual exchange is understood as an exchange of love on the part of the man for sexual service on the part of the woman. "That's it," she says, "it was a practice that allowed me to hide my body, to have a man in love at my feet but not at all a real sexual fantasy." Her interview shows the influence of the gynarchist speeches and media on the question of whether it is legitimate for a male sub and a female dominant to have sexual intercourse: the phenomenon is addressed that a dominant woman would leave her position of power during sexual intercourse, because after all she is the one who is penetrated. In her case, those discourses are interpreted and appropriated so that they agree with the own designs of the practitioners and allow her to reinvent herself as a "super chick" in an illusion of power, which allows her to erase faults and fragilities. The recourse to gynarchy as an entry into BDSM sexuality then traces the contours of a self that lacks originality and authenticity and is similar to a false self. Sonia's interview shows that it is possible to enter this world and to have practices linked to female domination without having any prior fantasy or any knowledge of the practices. For a long time, Sonia uses the gynarchist universe and the BDSM practices to avoid confronting what is problematic for her: her body, her lack of self-confidence, and her lack of love. She then becomes a particularly vulnerable partner for a "souminator," that is to say, for a man who imposes his own fantasies on her – under the pretext of submission – and settles as a parasite in her life. Sonia, from this point of view, embodies the contradiction between the omnipotent image of the unattainable dominatrix and the instrumentalization of female sexuality by the submissive men.

Instead of the freedom that the masochistic contract is supposed to offer to women, we can be confronted with a form of generalized subjection that is not unrelated to the emergence of mental alienation. This arbitrary form of the contract they had is that of a closed world that thwarts the movements of empathy. This relationship, which is caught up in the idealization of the fantasy mother, cannot hope for a transformation of the power relations because no adaptation with Sonia's personality is possible because playing the role of goddess implies for her lover to deny her vulnerability and her phallic jouissance, and to "never question himself and threaten to flee as soon as she goes wrong." I point out to Sonia that the form of the sessions she was having with her partner is similar to those found in venal relationships. They have a beginning and an end. They begin at the initiative of the submissive, and the dominant must be dressed according to the ideal of the Domina in boots and leather. Here, her sexuality is codified in such a way that she avoids any form of unexpectedness or slippage. If following a protocol has the advantage of avoiding being destabilized by her own drives, it leads her to a progressive tolerance for an organization of the script, which goes against her desires, her needs, and her health since she has fallen into a nervous breakdown and ends up meeting her partner's demands under the threat that he will leave her and she will lose her nanny too. The mistress ends up in the place of the slave whose desires can never be fulfilled because it is to her care (*care giving*) alone that he owes the ability to transcend slavery. The gynarchist work, as it is conceived, has a dimension in which individuals, acting or not, can get lost or be alienated. In fact, the gynarchist theories based on Bachofen's theories of matriarchy insist on the mother–child dyad. This is divorced from reality. The mother–child relationship is always embedded in a network of relationships that contribute to the educational work. The mother does not raise her child alone, even if she is the head of the family. To limit care to this relationship is to obscure everything that converges to designate the mother as the main person responsible for the child's well-being (Molinier et al. 2009: 17). They, thus, reinforce the prejudice that the nature of women is linked to the quality of care. It is not the sensitivity to suffering that is pathogenic, but the impossibility to express it. Yet, care is an activity that requires above all "to go back from the state of puppet to that of inhabited body" (Pankow 2004: 198); otherwise, one must face a dimension of exploitation and alienation for the caregiver.

3.6 Discussion

Researchers on BDSM relations in the tradition of Foucault (Foucault 1994: 743) have largely demonstrated that the analysis of power relations must be dissociated from S/M practices. In particular, the notion of play is used to dissociate

BDSM relations from power relations. They consider that, in order to protect their mental equilibrium, the practitioners of these types of practices must be able to distinguish between their played performances and the power relations in everyday life, to distance themselves from the relations of domination, and in short, to deconstruct for themselves what it is about the play and the violence in their relations (Spengler 1979: 58). However, when formulated in this way, some members of the community, including the gynarchist participants, do not recognize themselves; as Benoit argues, "I am not playing." They want to say that they take seriously what they are doing. One can understand them. Dividing play/reality in this way, one has the feeling that subjectivity would be split into two: an authentic part (that of the daily life) and an inauthentic part (that of the game). This remains valid for circumscribing a type of activity that consists in controlling and shaping one's own emotions and those of others. But it does not allow us to analyze the psychic processes that BDSM practices mobilize, and a fortiori sexuality in general. Understanding these processes requires a psycho-dynamic frame of reference, the concepts of psychological suffering, the unconscious, and defenses. The psyche of BDSM practitioners is not a docile tool, but it is more often an internal threat – the numerous anxieties and phobias of the fantasists who flee from the appointments I gave them testify to this. The unconscious also "works." What we experience in an intimate setting does not end in the bedroom but continues to affect us when we let go of our lover and can even affect our relationships in the workplace.

It is well known that crises in the couple lead to not only a decrease in productivity at work but also the loss of meaning in one's work that one would perform like an automaton influences sexuality. This can lead to a decrease in investment or, on the contrary, to an over-investment in sexuality. For a concrete subject, work and private life are in competition and constantly interact. In particular, the subjective time of work tends to overflow the objective time that is allocated to them. We know that the subjective time of involvement in salaried work or in domestic work and private concerns does not reduce to the objective time, the one that is counted, measured by hours and minutes, and divided into sequences by schedules (Legarreta 2008).

In a gynarchist context, the relationship between work and sexuality is complicated. Domestic work would function as another "stage" for the realization of fantasies, where the permeability between domestic work and private life appears as an essential component of the gynarchist lifestyle. The organization of domestic work and gynarchist way of life would come in this philosophy of life to be added to the other one in a "complementary" way. The subjective time of the fantasy, which can go as far as invading daily time and even work, proves to be double-edged. On the one hand, these fantasies and dreams are rich and conducive to the development of ingenious practices; on the other hand, they also tend to compromise the possibilities of extracting oneself from erotic life, and concentrating and devoting oneself to something else. Thus, the subjective time of the gynarchist fantasy can be experienced as a defense in the psychological register, as Henry's case shows. Following the protocol to the letter can then be particularly problematic. The absence of a divide between private life and work can prevent awareness of the violence of the relationship, which is eroticized. Practitioners like Henry can multiply defensive behaviors to try to make breaks in a particularly painful continuity.

Following the protocol "to the letter" can oblige the female practitioners to hide the pleasure taken in a genital sexuality and desires of submissiveness that they nevertheless practice, in order to follow the gynarchist way of life (management of the gap between the conception of gynarchy and the reality of these relationships). The gynarchist writings centered on the desire of the men, and the women like Sonia can decide to adopt this way of life without sexual fantasy of domination. Sexuality becomes confused with work, generating feelings of strangeness, violence in private life, and even emotional exhaustion (burnout).

In these cases, there would be a violence in the personal life and a real difficulty for the exhausted subject to distance himself from what he lives. Everyone is thus progressively called upon to participate in a distorted and embellished description of reality, which obscures not only feminine pleasure but also reality. Thus, the protocols threaten to deviate more and more from the reality of the relationships and the exchange that builds them.

As a matter of fact, the experience of the real "is also a subjective experience of failure, of uncertainty, of impotence, of doubt" (Dejours 2006: 128). The feedback on experience does not only consist in exhibiting one's exploits but also in speaking about one's failures, through which the resistance to technical mastery is revealed. But to speak about it is also to take the risk of being considered incompetent and critical toward the gynarchist worldview, especially when one reports an experience that contradicts the alleged mastery attested by the protocols. If the authentic experience of the world becomes incommunicable, this situation can turn tragic. It can lead someone, for example, to doubt security, safety, or the fact of being in a healthy relationship. This person can find himself or herself alone and disavowed or can become the target of psychological manipulation like it is the case with Henry. He then finds himself in a psychologically scabrous position: either under the effect of the other's disavowal, he ends up doubting the validity of his experience and then risks depression, or he continues with his nose to the grindstone to follow the protocol and is then threatened by the deleterious effects of the work overload and risks drifting toward emotional burnout. The risk is reinforced for participants who have weak connections with people identifying as gynarchist. However, this time spent on exchanges is indispensable for participants to elaborate what they experience, to give meaning to their practice, and to weave together the fine web of experiences, rejections, attractions, and normative agreements on what is appropriate to do.

The particular interaction that takes place between work and private life in gynarchist relationships and the difficulties this interplay entails make it apparent that the distance with the protocol is an essential component of mental health. Mistress Sandra talks about her relationship with Benoit, a relationship in which she feels fulfilled. Spontaneity in the exchange is the crucible of the good distance with the protocol. The love passion of Mistress Sandra and Benoit is for us the index of a certain relation to the other, which includes, among many obstacles, the possibility of an emancipation from alienation, when the lover withdraws in front of the object of his desire in order to possess it in another way. The story of Mistress Sandra and Benoit shows us that a collective work of elaboration of the sexual practices carried out throughout the relationship in a perspective articulating ideal of the self and subjective moral autonomy can succeed in re-elaborating the repressed contents of the "original" phantasm, which then return to them enriched with a new life. Elusive as an object, the other is never for all a simple source of disappointment that brings the subject back to himself. The recognition of the other can be anticipated if the essential is done in the narcissistic support of love and work. Mistress Sandra supports the creative work of her lover. Their practices allow a conception of a sexual act inside a system in which the desire of the submissive men plays an important role in the construction of a fulfilled, safe, sane and secure relationship. It could even be that this work would favor the emergence of a new ethic of intimacy thanks to the virtue of mutual erotic care.

> We're always thinking about making new things, we're making my cellar, he wants to get tied up in the cellar so bad. He's taking things in that direction. But I don't feel pushed because I like it. He is just interested in me. He is transparent. He is only with me. There is imagination, there are ideas that come up. It happens on the spot or because we want to make things together as the Plexiglas to crush the testicles between two mirrors and two Plexiglas, we make objects, decorations, places both. We do a lot of things together. We will hang chains on trees with rings, the last time we had mounted a swing and things like that, bamboo poles on the ground to put someone in a cross according to the imagination that we can have together. We talk about our sessions to know how it went or about the security. It is a sharing, it can come from one or the other.

His status as an alter ego makes him rather an inexhaustible source of learning about herself and of understanding the experience they have lived together. By working together, they bring to life living associations and institute pacts of sociality, whose most codified character always betrays the same concern to ensure the stable bases of a link that the subject needs to pose as indelible in order to be able to pose himself. The gynarchist relation of Mistress Sandra and Benoit is full of joyful stories, because their trajectory of emancipation weaves successfully sexuality and work. Thus, some gynarchists, by preparing the scenarios together, blur the lines and allow for the staging of sexuality and the participation in gynarchic culture (expressed through do-it-yourself games) to be considered together. Indeed, the experiences of Mistress Sandra show her love for a man who would also be a carrier of the values of care, thus calling for a form of reciprocity in the concern (of the desire) of the other.

> I was more fulfilled with this man than with all the others before because he is always there. We grow together all the time. We push each other in our personal development, in our work, in our projects, personally. I have never seen a man who does everything to make me rich. That's what he tells me, all I want is for you to get rich all the time, at all levels, whatever I decide. While I've always been told why you do this, always reproaches, there is never anything. It is a total happiness. I have feelings just talking about it, I have never seen that anywhere else, especially for a daily life. It is exceptional. It's all the time attention to make me feel good, the laundry is always done, I don't lack anything.

Thus, considering the moral dimension of the activities performed together pushes us to reconsider the importance of care in its multiple deployments, and to refuse to associate the figure of the caregiver with a fixed gendered identity. This dimension also pushes us to detach care from an idealized image of the mother that gynarchist fantasies support. But it also invites us to criticize the dichotomy between men, "the real ones" with whom women could consider a romantic relationship, and the others, the so-called "carpet men" (discriminatory terms that are sometimes used to describe submissive men). This reciprocity at the heart of the heterosexual relationship of Sandra and Bastien makes this less material and impalpable dimension of sexuality appear that Teresa de Lauretis called practice of love.

The reference to a defensive ideology is the most constraining aspect in this form of sexuality. Its revelation in love addiction offers on the contrary "a chance to develop a new ethic of intimacy allowing the loving partners to cultivate the erotic and moral values of care and mutual attention of life together, with equal rights and expectations" (Pharo 2015: 9).

Notes

1 With Spengler, I define subculture as a social system in which valid social norms of behavior are different from the main frame of reference. This frame of reference confirms and allows deviant behavior (Spengler 1979).

2 https://obeywomen.pink/female-supremacy-university/

3 https://www.youtube.com/channel/UCq9riLMNHt4hAvr635XCciA

4 The idealization of the self requires the idealization of the object, and the stake of the idealization is the secondary narcissism, the love of oneself. The self is constituted in the identification to the objects of love and repatriates secondarily the qualities of the loved and idealized object in the self (Molinier 2006: 166).

5 http://www.femdom-resource.com/femdom-artwork/

6 https://www.nanshakh.com/fsp3.htm

7 The core of masochism, according to Krafft-Ebing, consists more in the fantasies than in the practices of submission – the practices only externalizing the fantasies.

8 https://dominamag.com/suprematie-feminine/vive-la-gynarchie-debut-dune-relation-flr/
9 The subjective moral autonomy is a subjective capacity that belongs to the field of the dianetic virtues, in the sense that it mobilizes jointly the intellectual exercise and the practical wisdom (phronesis).

Bibliography

Agamben G. (1998). *Stanze*. Paris, Rivages, Poche.
Bachofen J. J. (1996). *Le droit maternel. Recherche sur la gynécocratie de l'Antiquité dans sa nature religieuse et politique,* trad. et préf. par É. Barilier, Lausanne, L'Âge d'homme.
Bisson L. (1999). *Chaucer and the Late Medieval World*. London, Macmillan Press.
d'Arbrant A. (1997). *La Gynarchie et les aventures de Wandine*. Paris, Diachroniques.
Dejours C. (2006). Aliénation et clinique du travail. *Actuel Marx*, 1(39), 123–144. doi: 10.3917/amx.039.0123; https://www.cairn.info/revue-actuel-marx-2006-1-page-123.htm
Dejours C. (2009). *Travail vivant. 1: Sexualité et travail*. Paris, Petite Bibliotheque Payot.
Dejours C. (2015) 1993. *Travail: Usure mentale*. Paris, Bayard.
De Lauretis T. (1990). Eccentric Subjects: Feminist Theory and Historical Consciousness, [en ligne]. *Feminist Studies*, 16(1), 115–150. Disponible.
Deleuze G. (1967). *Présentation de Sacher-Masoch, Le froid et le cruel*. Paris, Les éditions de minuit.
Deremetz A. (2018). *Die BDSM-Szene: Eine Ethnographische Feldstudie*. Gießen, Psychosozial Verlag.
Foucault M. (1994) 1979. Une interview: Sexe, pouvoir et la politique de l'identité. In M. Foucault (Ed.), *Dits et Écrits 1954–1988*, 735–746. Paris, Gallimard.
Freud S. (1924). *Ma vie et la psychanalyse*. Paris, Gallimard.
Harris A. (2015). *The Training Farm: A Journey into Submission*. North Charleston, [Harris CreateSpace Independent Publishing Platform.
Hart L. (2003). *La performance sadomasochiste: Entre corps et chair*. Paris, EPEL.
Krafft-Ebing R. von (1895) 1983. *Psychopathia Sexualis*, trad. 8Eme éd. allemande, E. Laurent, S. Scapo, G. Carré, Paris, Carré.
Lacan J. (1967). *L'angoisse. Lecon VII. Séance du 16 janvier 1963*. Paris, Seuil.
Lacan J. (1969). *Le Séminaire, Livre XVI, D'un à l'autre, séminaire du 19 Mars 1969*. Paris, Seuil.
Lacan J. (1972–1973). *Le Séminaire, Livre XX*. Paris, Seuil, 1975.
Lacan J. (1986). *L'éthique de la psychanalyse, Le séminaire, Livre 7*. Paris, Seuil.
Lacan J. (2001). 1960–1961. *Le Séminaire, Livre VIII, Le transfert*. Paris, Seuil.
Lane R. (2016). *Finding Love through Female Domination*. Bloomington, IN, Xlibris.
Laplanche J., Pontalis J. B. (1998). *Fantasme originaire. Fantasmes des origines. Origines du fantasme*. Paris, Hachette.
Legarreta M. (2008). El tiempo donado el en ámbito doméstico. Reflexiones para el análisis del trabajo doméstico y los cuidados. *Cuadernos de Relaciones Laborales*, 26(2) (à paraître), 106–112.
Molinier P. (2006). *Les enjeux psychiques du travail*. Paris, Payot.
Molinier P., Laugier S., Paperman P. (2009). *Qu'est-ce que le care. Souci des autres, sensibilité, responsabilité*. Paris, Petite Bibliotheque Payot.
Nanshakh. (2022). *Gynarchistan, the country of full employment* [Nanshakh, drawing]. www.nanshakh.com
Pankow G. (2004). *Structure Familiale et Psychose*. Paris, Flammarion.
Pharo P. (2015). *La dépendance amoureuse: Attachement, passion, addiction*. Paris, PUF.

Popa D. (2014). Subjectivation et mélancolie. La fonction des fantasmes dans les stratégies de la perte. Université catholique de Louvain. *Meta: Research in Hermeneutics, Phenomenology, and Practical Philosophy*, VI(1), 151–174. ISSN 2067-3655, www.metajournal.org

Ritter A. (2021). *No Escape from Matria*. Washington, DC, Kindle edition: Binding Erotic Books.

Sacher-Masoch L. von (2009). *La Vénus à la fourrure*. Paris, Payot. First edition in 1924.

Sacher-Masoch W. von (2014). *Confession de ma vie*. Paris, Rivages poche/Petite bibliothèque.

Sardax. (2006). *The Art of Sardax*. London, The Erotic Print Society.

Scott G. G. (1997). *Erotic Power. An Exploration of Dominance and Submission. Secaucus*. New York, Citadel.

Spengler A. (1979). *Sadomasochisten und Ihre Subkulturen*. Frankfurt/New York, Campus Verlag.

Tin L.-G. (2008). *L'invention de l'hétérosexuelle*. Paris, Éditions Autrement.

Vivès J. (2011). L'amour courtois entre fauteuil et divan: pour une lecture poétique de l'amour de transfert. *Cliniques Méditerranéennes*, 84, 9–18. https://doi.org/10.3917/cm.084.0009

Wetzstein, T. A., Steinmetz, L., Reis, C., Eckert, R. (1993). *Sadomasochismus Szenen und Rituale*. Hamburg, Rowohlt Tachenbuch Verlag.

Winnicott D. W. (1975). *Jeu et realité, l'espace potentiel*. Paris, Gallimard.

Websites

Female Supremacy University: https://obeywomen.pink/female-supremacy-university/
Gynarchy Rules: https://www.youtube.com/channel/UCq9riLMNHt4hAvr635XCciA
Le blog suprematiefeminine: http://suprematiefeminine-o2.erog.fr/#

4

NEIGHBORHOOD DOMINAS AND PIGEONS

An intersectional approach to financial slavery on Facebook

4.1 Introduction

I became aware of money slavering by coincidence. *I did not at first try to analyze this sexual practice.* In fact, I had never heard about it before first creating an account to observe female domination on Facebook. Studying female domination on social networks allows me to grasp current practices by considering the development of Internet use, the frequency of connections, and the importance of using social networks to meet people in BDSM environments. Sexuality on the net offers the possibility of testing new fantasy scenarios thanks to virtuality as "money slavering," which is an anglicism used by the French BDSM communities online. Given the existence of "slaver" as a verb in English meaning drool, the term "slavering" in English can be problematic, and I will, therefore, for the purpose of this chapter, replace it with "financial slavery."[1] Financial slavery can be defined as an essentially virtual form of domination, where a man is supposed to derive pleasure from a woman by satisfying her financially. It is a sexual practice I watched growing for about 15 years in the French-speaking online BDSM communities and is very widespread on Facebook.

From a political perspective, I wanted to examine the social vulnerabilities provoked by the influence of Facebook upon BDSM subcultures by documenting its commercial exploitation. Gayle Rubin already highlighted the commercial exploitation of BDSM while documenting the difference between the old guard and the new guard of BDSM. According to her, this change in the BDSM scene became evident in the 1980s at public parties.[2] But we also notice that in a neoliberalist economy dominated by digital technology, "where each and every event and situation in life can be given a value on the market" (Vogl 2013: 152), mediums like Facebook play a crucial role in inciting people who were initially just curious about BDSM, to sell their services as a "money mistress." Thus, professional

DOI: 10.4324/9781003258537-6

domination still exists in its classical forms – in salons – but new social networks have led to the emergence of new forms of sex work. For women who wish to use domination for profit, Internet networks and specialized BDSM discussion groups are suitable niches in which they can easily function without the risk of physical contact with clients (Lugand 2017). We consequently witness the spread of new fantasies connected to *femdom*, alongside the proliferation of profiles of "venal" dominatrixes. This has to do with the relative ease of selling sexual services online: one just needs a bank account, an Internet connection, and a webcam.

Social networks like Facebook function as a marketplace in which people come together in ever more specialized subcultures according to sexual interests (Wetzstein et al. 1993) and where money in online BDSM practices is merely the manifestation of a deeper dynamic of social marginalization and alienation. While Weiss postulates that represented BDSM enthusiasts are frequently white, embodying the bourgeois values – the access to capital, both cultural and monetary (Weiss 2011) – I argue that online sexual practices with the introduction of new practitioners who often come from working-class and/or non-white backgrounds may introduce broad new relations and tensions between "consumerism and desire; race, class, and neoliberalism; politics and privilege." At the same time, groups against financial slavery appeared. I could not be indifferent to the hate speech conveyed by the money mistresses practicing financial slavery. It has become recurrent in the *money slave* groups on Facebook, as attested by the formation of groups to denounce those practices and criticize the women practicing it. By examining the insults and verbal violence uttered by BDSM practitioners against young women practicing financial slavery – called money mistresses – often from working-class or non-white backgrounds, I will show how an ideal of a dominant woman (based on the model of a bourgeois white woman) is constructed by contrast. On this point, I interpret the work of putting forward the image of dominant women on Facebook, as well as the attitudes adopted as a defense to fight against the whore stigma that turns out to occupy a central place in the erotic economy between submissive men and dominant women. Dominant women seek to impose an "honorable" representation of the ideal dominatrix by making a work of distance in their relation to the money.

The spread of online sexual services is related to the growing importance of the service sector that characterizes the new work organizations. It has led many authors to focus on the "mobile, and even 'flexible' in the neoliberal sense, characteristics of gender identities produced by service activities" (Molinier 2006: 277). In this sense, this chapter highlights how the fantasies born in this new economic form play strategically with gender. Financial slavery, as a fantasy scenario of typically heterosexual and male submission, is similar to other practices of female domination in that men and women are supposed to occupy the opposite position to that which is assigned to them in the gender order through the subversion of the whore stigma. However, can we talk about subversion of gender relations? Practiced in France by many young women of African and North African origin, from working-class backgrounds, it reveals the interweaving of heterosexual sexuality with class and race hierarchies. Thus, this new form of "sexual relationship" that crystallizes around verbal violence and is characterized by the absence of the other's body accounts for the fixity of social identities of gender, sex, race, and class through subjectivity. I will also analyze how the absence of touch impedes the formation of subjectivity and diversity.

Judging from their Facebook walls, some dominatrixes had to stop working because of the impact of the COVID-19 pandemic lockdown and then had more time for their activities as money mistresses and more time to recruit clients. It is difficult to evaluate the importance of the practice. The fact that this praxis has been practiced over this long period of time and is today practiced in regions as far as Benin leads me to believe that we face a phenomenon that is not ephemeral.

4.2 BDSM subculture on Facebook: the power of images

The people I first spoke with on Facebook were not only interested in talking about their interest in BDSM, but they also wanted to share the way they discovered the BDSM community on Facebook, like Henry, 47 years old, a computer scientist. When I met Henry on Facebook, he was not doing very well with his social life, and he had submissive fantasies, but little success in realizing them. He had difficulty finding any dominant woman who wanted an affair with him. During a face-to-face interview, he revealed to me the experiences he had had with dominatrixes, most of whom were professionals and dominated him in exchange for money. For a while, he was "tripping" that way. Thanks to his technical and technology competence he has had the chance to weave a network of friends and therefore a network of power (action) within a community.

> It was a bit of an apprenticeship, discovering this world. I created this account on Facebook and at the same time, I created this kinky account, a fetishist pervert. So I oriented it really like that at first, it was only to meet people like that ... And the pictures ... The idea came because one day I went out with a girl who loved to take pictures and then the pictures were liked. So, I thought to myself: why not ... So I continued like that to take pictures of girlfriends and they were liked more and more. And then your account goes up, your site increases more and more, people trust you, they see that you are someone rather nice, funny, that you are not looking to fuck any chick so people enjoy it anyhow. That being said, I met a lot of girls thanks to that, when I say the best dating site, it was Facebook, doing that.

New rules of the game are appearing due to the importance of social networks. While people's notoriety previously relied primarily on their involvement in BDSM communities, some people have managed to gain notoriety by boosting their popularity on Facebook using their ability to play with images and to exercise their creative control over the images.

The specificity of interactions on the Internet is the overall usage of self-representation. Posting pics of body parts on the wall plays a crucial role in the interactions of money mistresses with submissive men on many levels. Deesse Noire told me that she enjoys posting photos of herself and that she does it for her own pleasure, highlighting a dimension of autoerotism in this practice. She adds that she does that for practical reasons: "As a matter of fact, it gives confidence to the submissives who are unaware of the fake content propagated in the social networks. By posting, they believe, I'm proving that I'm real!" but posting sexy pictures is also a way to get the submissive's attention and to keep him under control. In order to control a slave, K. "simply sends him pictures of what to buy with his money, or pictures of his feet so that he comes back quite easily." She explains that this energizes the general humiliation, "that moneyslaves like to be talked down to, made fun of for their dick size, insults, etc."

Within the BDSM community, the ideal of femininity put forward in female domination defines a set of values, attributes, behaviors, and attitudes that are socially valued and opposed to the attributes of the whore, from which they distinguish themselves by avoiding, among other things, publicly showing certain parts of their body. Thus, a great part of the images diffused by the money mistresses limits the representation of their bodies to these fetishes that are the feet, the legs.

4.3 Financial slavery as sex work

In this form of venal domination, men are expected to enjoy being insulted, denigrated, mocked, and ultimately "pigeonholed" by women they serve and financially satisfy. These financial rape games are also known as CNC, which stands for consensual non-consent. Although it varies from scene to scene, it is generally an extreme power exchange where, based on prior negotiation, there is "a victim" defeated by "a predator" through force. These practices involve the broadcasting of photos and short videos by the dominatrixes, hourly paid domination sessions on webcam, gift giving, mainly via Amazon, from lists drawn up by the money mistresses and broadcast on their wall to the submissives, or even the giving of money through participation in fundraising.

Because these practices often remain virtual, the line between reality and fiction can often become blurred, and it can be problematic to distinguish between play and reality of an insult. It is recognized in the BDSM community that such a distinction is necessary to differentiate BDSM practitioners from violent and abusive people (Baatz 1993). However, as Sanders argues, sex workers often create identities manufactured specifically for the workplace as a self-protective mechanism to deal with the stress of selling sex as well as to shape the image of the work as a business strategy to attract and maintain clients (Sanders 2005). In our study, financial slavery also lends itself to all sorts of cover-ups and pretense. K., for example, mentioned that although she had no bad experiences, people online "can hide behind their computers" and take advantage of this situation to "insult" and make "false promises." She says many submissives she meets online don't keep their word or show up for appointments.

But money slavering also involves face-to-face practices. According to K., the most common practices are the "plan dab" and the "cash meet." The first consists of "taking" the submissive's credit card:

> They give their code and I use an amount defined in advance, or not, if the submissive is a "player," after which he thanks us for taking his money and leaves. The cash meet takes a little longer. The submissive meets me at a location and may kiss my feet or lick my heels for ten minutes, then give me money.

The practices require the money mistress to strategically display "sadistic" emotions, such as indifference, superiority, and disdain, and as in any professional domination session, she negotiates with clients about what will happen. Both parties discuss the clients' desires and boundaries as well as the rules and limits set by the money mistress. BlackM expresses the critical importance of following her rules by exclaiming, "Take it or leave it!" For her part, before any session, K. takes the time to converse with the slave she is going to dominate:

> We'll talk about what he likes, what his fetishes are, how he prefers me to take care of him, and if we're going to go to the dab plan; we'll set a limit on how much money he can withdraw, for example, $600 maximum, or if we're going to go on a shopping spree, we'll set a budget for him to stick to with his credit card.

Both women interviewed described feelings such as empathy and respect they have for the money slaves, reminding us that they are aware that it is first and foremost a game. BlackM says that the compassion she shows behind the scenes as a money mistress also permeates her interactions on stage. She mentions working with "rare and exceptional" slaves, some of whom she has met regularly or for a few years. She seeks to grow and learn through interaction with these men whose "crazy sexual fantasies" make her curious. One can then assume that in some cases, especially when money mistresses develop a regular clientele over the long term, the money mistress–money slave relationship may lead to friendship or a personal relationship, which could complicate the relationship between front- and backstage (Goffman 1959; Levey and Pinsky 2015a). In contrast, K., like many other "pro-doms," imposes "boundaries with severe restrictions on who can socialize with [her] outside of sessions" (Levey and Pinsky 2015a), more in line with the norms of the money slavering power dynamic: K. does not socialize with any money slaves outside of paid sessions.

4.4 Ostracization of the neighborhood dominas by authorized members of BDSM

The "neighborhood dominas" are young women who uphold their North African origins through nicknames such as Queens of the Orient and Mistresses

Sophia and Eloise or are active in groups such as Maghreb Queens and Algerian Dominatrixes. The marginalization of the neighborhood dominas by the "authorized" members of the BDSM community involves a collaboration between certain white men and women around the definition of the ideal dominatrix. A racist "common sense" persuades white men and women that money mistresses are "rabble" [*racaille*][3] and defines them with this term. According to Patricia, money mistresses lack respect for the submissives they have. They are only interested in money, and they have no respect for the BDSM values upon which a session should be based. Some people even argue that those practitioners aren't doing BDSM because the money mistresses are not aware that they can endanger a submissive in his physical integrity and his psychological integrity and are not taking responsibility for their actions.

Indeed, BDSM practices are defined by the values of reciprocity, trust, and commitment underpinning the traditional BDSM communities and subcultures (Miller and Devon 1995; Wiseman 1996; Scott 1997; Moser and Madeson 2002). Would mixing money with sexual practice undermine its values? In any case, the use of money in online BDSM practices is one point of crystallization of a deeper dynamic of marginalization and social alienation. According to Jaqueline, the dominettes would abuse the trust, the credulity, and the submission drives of these men. She explains her aversion to money mistresses by the idea that these women would give a "bad image of BDSM to a lot of young submissives who will then think that they have to pay to talk to a dominatrix." Thus, according to her, a dominatrix should show a lack of interest in money. She thus expresses disdain and contempt "for those who are more obviously stigmatized" than herself (Goffman 1959: 107). It seems that maintaining an "us versus them" attitude toward money mistresses is how these dominatrixes mitigate their own association with the stigma of the whore (Pheterson 2001). This is reminiscent of Levey and Pinsky's (2015a) observation that professional dominatrixes cultivate their difference in relation to women who have sex with their clients. As G. Pheterson notes, the whore has nothing to do with the commerce of sex per se; the whore is always the Other. In this regard, Jackeline also values her difference from money mistresses: although she too charges for online domination sessions, she claims that she does not need this to make a living, as she has a side job. She developed tactics to differentiate herself from professional dominatrixes such as stopping the sessions at a specific time but continuing as long as "you enjoy yourself."

However, it is hard to figure out how Jaqueline knows that the women she speaks about do not care about those values and are solely interested in money since her strong aversion toward those women had prevented her from engaging in a conversation with them. Indeed, it doesn't reflect the discourse of the money mistresses I spoke with and the two I interviewed. *These money mistresses would certainly be unable to recognize themselves based on the description given by Jaqueline.* That being said, as "authorized" members of the BDSM community, Jaqueline speaks with certain white men and women about the definition of the ideal dominatrix versus the stigmatization of those considered "rabble" [*racaille*]. This stigmatization is supported by the elements of violence that appear in some BDSM practices. It is precisely the elements of violence that appear in money slavering that make the distinction and also the mixture of play and seriousness at the same time problematic for her. Certain elements of violence, in particular homophobic insults that appear in money slavering (sissy, faggot, poof), lead to debate and discourse on the border between play and reality. Philippe, for example, maintains that these insults convey homophobia, something he does not support. It is interesting to notice that while certain elements of violence, in particular homophobic insults, are questioned, others elements of violence like misogynistic insults or animalization are used in his practice. For instance, on a wall, Philippe was baptized: dirty little whore.

However, the "invisibilization" of the money mistresses during their discourses is not conscious, and then the violence exercised cannot be assumed. The symbolic violence of the term "rabble" depends on the degree of its visibility in the social space and the complicity it has created between people (Puaud 2012). The racist imagery that accompanies the stigmatization of the money mistress is essential to the construction of the invisibilization of the dominated. In 2010, the term *racaille* is regularly reactivated and/or implied in many political and media discourses (Puaud 2012). It has become recurrent in the *money slave* groups on Facebook, as attested by the formation of a group entitled "Stop Scum Money Slavering" [*Stop au money slavering en mode racaille*]. On the one hand, one can say that calling these young women *racaille* seems to encourage racial and whore-phobic slurs. We can see in any case an interaction between racial and gender discrimination. On the other hand, I would argue that these attitudes adopted to distinguish oneself from neighborhood dominas can be interpreted as a defense against overlapping stigmas – the stigma of whore, on the one hand, and the stigma attached to BDSM sexualities, on the other. These defenses put in place in order to deal with these intersections of stigmas (Levey and Pinsky 2015a) unfortunately inadvertently reproduce particular types of stigma. Thus, while informants like Jaqueline belong to subcultures that focus on "sex-positive" politics in an attempt to destigmatize non-normative sexuality, "their 'I'm not a money mistress' narratives potentially reify whore stigma instead of destigmatizing prostitution" (Levey and Pinsky 2015a). And I will add that this narrative potentially reifies whore stigma with any other stigma exercised against social minorities.

4.5 The practices of financial slavery from the point of view of the money slave

The sincerity of the engagement of any dominant women is often put into question. In fact, in my first month investigating, I spent less time with submissives I met online debating about their love for foot fetishism or leather, and more time attempting to persuade them that I was "a real" dominant woman sincerely interested in female domination. However, if the doubt of finding a dominant woman often leads submissive participants to use the service of professional dominatrixes (Scott 1997), the lack of interest of money mistresses for the practices and their partner is highlighted. According to Taoufik, the services they offer are often reduced to a minimum and, in a much less conventional way, these women express strongly their contempt or even hatred for their male partners. In addition, the dialogs between a *money mistress* and a *money slave* are purely utilitarian, completely devoid of any warmth, as the interview carried out with Taoufik shows: "Sadly, in most cases, it's simply an exchange of goods. A shared interest, financial for the woman, and for me to satisfy my drive, my need, my addiction."

Finally, it is worth noting that the description and scenario of "financial rape" according to Taoufik, as well as according to the representations produced by the money mistresses on their own social networks, emphasize the hard work of men, in contrast with the idleness and vanity of women: these characteristics seem to be part of the erotic scenarios of financial slavery. This seems to contradict the proclaimed subversion of power relations: these characteristics are likely to doubly reassure potential male clients, by exalting their traditional role as providers and denying the work done in return by money mistresses (Lugand et al. Forthcoming).

Indeed, despite such representations, the practices performed by money mistresses do involve an investment of time and money: for example, K. states that she invests materials (shoes and lingerie) in her practice. BlackM also mentions the research done on the Internet in order to "select the practices" that suit her. Through exchanges with her slaves, she seeks to learn more about their inclinations and desires. Finally, another large part of the work is emotional: K. mentions the work of "managing" and "putting up" with slaves who speak disrespectfully to her by taking advantage of the anonymity of the Internet, in order, she says, to "get insulted for free." She "blocks at least 20 of them a day on Facebook."

The work of the money mistresses thus seems to include a requirement of deletion to be effective. Indeed, the way in which the money mistresses represent their services – as if it were a scam – makes this work invisible and look like something other than work, namely a form of enjoyment, leisure, and the spontaneous expression of a personality trait or "nature." This demand for the invisibility of work has already been identified in the care work performed, for example, by cleaning ladies, childcare workers, or unpaid household help (Molinier et al. 2009).

The online content produced by money mistresses thus presents two paradoxes: for the money slave, the paradox of being both overtly humiliated in terms of his sexual prowess and subtly flattered in terms of his economic power, reinforcing that way his virility, the pillar of masculine defense, and for the money mistress, the paradox of a job that, in order to be sold, must first be denied as such, when they claim, in order to humiliate their partners, to receive remuneration in exchange for "nothing." These practices reflect the alienation of the female subjectivity in the stereotypes of the socially constructed. For example, K. highlights and advertises her feeling that as a lady she deserves to be gratified by presents from a gentleman. BlackM argues that she is a special woman and deserves to be treated as a princess. The attitudes exposed to assert themselves as dominant would thus paradoxically reinforce the feminine defense of muliebrity whose spring is the erasure of oneself through the invisibilization of its work.

4.6 The money mistress as a subaltern position

The narratives of Taoufik, Jaqueline, and other authorized members of BDSM perhaps consolidate the subaltern (Spivak[4]) position of the *money mistress* within the world of BDSM. I make the hypothesis that the articulation of the invisibilization of desire (through the prism of the whore stigma) and the invisibilization of work (through the lens of the separation of the sphere) is an important mechanism in the subaltern position of the money mistress. On the one hand, money mistresses are represented as objects which were talked about by Taoufik and other members of the BDSM community, but the assumptions made about what they think and how they do their sexual practices are constructed without taking into consideration their own voices. On the other hand, the sexual excitement and enjoyment that money mistresses obtain from financial slavery are not explicitly discussed. Represented as an object of desire, or abjection, their own desires are not mentioned or silenced. *The sincerity of their investment in BDSM is totally ignored*, or, in other words, the fact that they do it for pleasure (too) is denied (their interest is represented as purely economical and antithetical). In this sense, the prejudice according to which men have stronger sexual drives than women, to which Taoufik adheres, participates fully in the negation of the female sexual desire. The sexual desires of neighborhood money mistresses are not even questioned; they are totally invisible. The problem is that this does not reflect the discourse of the money mistresses I spoke with and interviewed. *These women would certainly be unable to recognize themselves using these examples.*

Both money mistresses I interviewed initially expressed financial disinterest while they were experiencing BDSM practices. According to Blackgoddess, "[A]t the beginning I did it for free especially out of passion and [then] I got to know some money slaves who take pleasure in being ripped off." But they also affirm that they rapidly began to enjoy it: for example, K. admits that the basic idea comes from the submissive who created the fantasy and paid the domina to realize it, but she also stresses that the money mistresses are active in the sexual scene and "add their pinch into it." Personally, she said, "I like to humiliate them with harsh words, making fun of the size of their dick, insult them, knowing that they like to be humiliated in that way as well." She said that her pleasure derived from the enjoyment she gives to the money slave. The sadistic pleasure of K. is also related to her *ability to refuse* a particular sexual practice (like genital sex), communication with the money slave, or gifts received.

> K.: For example, the submissive comes to deposit a sum at your feet and licks them for you. You will add your spice by telling him that a loser like

him cannot have this privilege. You will frustrate him and therefore add your pinch into it which will certainly please him and in the evening he will send you a message telling you that he wants more. You do with it what you want. It is flexible and anything goes.

Those pieces of interviews contradict the purely utilitarian, selfish view of the interaction between money mistresses and money slaves given by Taoufik. Money mistresses play an active role in the scenarios "adding their pinch into it."

Money mistresses also express the pleasure they feel in a much clearer way. Leila, a former dominette, describes her experiences when she was 18, pointing out that "when you start you quickly want to continue." The fact of being in a gang with other women would encourage the dominettes to go frankly in the "nastiness," in the cruelty. It is a question of showing to the others of what they are capable. Mistress K. expresses her "drive of money mistress," as well as her urge to "financially rape money slaves." She speaks about the "cerebral pleasure taken in those practices," "the enormous satisfaction to have a man under her feet," "to have a man ready for everything to get a bit of her attention," and the excitation felt while receiving a notification that she received 500 euros. This last statement helps us to understand that these desires and pleasures are not in themselves in contradiction with their interest in money: on the contrary, part of this desire emerges from the exchange of money, and the very practice of financial slavery consists in not respecting a supposed separation between the sexual impulse and the economic exchange.

Yet, the analysis of Taoufik on financial slavery continues to conform to a psychological expression of sexuality, while the sexual drives are naturalized as an irrepressible male need and rationalized as vital for our economy, which transforms these needs into a "market" (Altman 2001). Thus, men like Taoufik, more so than women, are more likely to take their desires and sexual drives seriously and invest money in them. On the contrary, the whore stigma still threatens women not to express their desire openly and to present it in a publicly acceptable manner. Here it is by working on the limits in their relationship with money that they can defend themselves most effectively against this stigma. This is all the truer for the (traditional) dominatrix, whose "upper-class" membership or appearance should ideally signify that she is indifferent to the appeal of money. This stigmatization that affects and burns the dominettes that would not have respected its limits cannot at the same time threaten to label them as profiteers, venal women, but also it makes it possible to rejuvenate the prejudices according to which "women generally think less about the sexual questions than the men" (Scott 1997: 28). But this point of view does not only silence their own voices, but it also denies that there can be something strongly erotic about exchanges of money (Lugand et al. Forthcoming).

4.7 The subversion of the whore stigma in the fantasy of financial slavery

What is striking in financial slavering is that it emphasizes the precariousness of the self and its vulnerabilities, not as a danger of destruction of the self and its identity certainties, but as a constantly renewed resource.[5] Taoufik eroticizes the racialized perception and interpretation of himself and his relationship to sexuality by these young women.

> Taoufik: I am Moroccan, from a wealthy background, and belong to a much more valued and socially integrated class than these young suburban girls, so with these girls, I have the pleasure of being, at the same time, white, rich, and French, or I'm treated like a shitty little Arab by native French Women and that excites me too, or I'm treated as a Moroccan dog by the Algerians, given the rivalry between Moroccans and Algerians. In either case, I win.

Thus, in order to grasp the specificity of financial slavery with Taoufik, I had to confront racial and class-based reality in France. In fact, it is within this unequal structure – and because of its inequality – that Taoufik's masochistic desire finds its place, as a man dominant in terms of gender and social class, but dominated as a non-white man living and working in Paris:

> Taoufik:... I find it more humiliating to be humiliated by a person who is supposed to be socially, physically, and intellectually weaker and it's this power reversal that is very humiliating. I've even spoken about intellectual, social and physical inferiority and I would even add an ethnic inferiority, meaning that many native French men [*français de souche*] are attracted to the "neighbourhood dominas."

Taoufik has a hybrid status, both complicit and subjugated from the perspective of the dominant socially constructed form of masculinity, the hegemonic masculinity.[6] Although Taoufik, as a non-white male from an ex-French colony who practices BDSM sexuality where he is the bottom, is excluded from hegemonic masculinity, his interview suggests that sometimes non-hegemonic masculinities can exist in tension with hegemonic masculinity for the same individual.

Because it does not involve personalized relationships, the virtual scene appears as a suitable space to play upon these contradictions. It helps him play upon different masochistic scenarios in order to "win." Depending on what the interaction requires, he can identify with the white man when speaking with a young, underprivileged, North African woman, or with the "shitty little Arab" when speaking to a "native" Frenchwoman. In all these configurations, Taoufik chooses a discursive position most likely to fuel the erotization of shame and powerlessness. The relationships between the submissives and the "neighborhood dominas" are therefore characterized by an economic, cultural, and racial asymmetry.

The "neighborhood dominas" do not "dominate" men in the same way as white women would. Their *money slavering* practices are based on role-playing, which reinforces the intersection between gender, class, and race, as attested by the images shared by Reine Marok'haine[7] "which are a good reflection of [her] way of thinking": a fair-haired man (hegemonic white masculinity) serving an Arab woman. Deesse Noire asserts that most white men she spoke with dream about being dominated by a black woman.[8] This racial dimension is embedded in her identity as a dominant woman. She told me that she deserves to be worshipped because she is a Black woman who likes to be respected. On the other hand, K. describes this type of role-playing as fetishism: "While some slaves worship black women, others are submissive to Arab women." Many submissives, like Patrick with whom I chatted on Facebook, justify their preference because they find them more easily cruel, vindictive.

They find their desire for revenge more realistic. According to Amber Jamila Musser, black women are denied the opportunity to occupy a subjugated position when they are immediately seen as members of an essential category inscribed in the historical narrative of slavery, whose performance becomes symptomatic (Musser 2014). K. doesn't like the term "racial domination," and she doesn't like to play with that dimension herself: "It doesn't change much for me if a white man worships me because I am a woman or come from the Maghreb. That is more in the head of the money slave this fantasy." Thus, money slaves think of racialized women like K. or Blackgoddess, first and foremost, as representatives of a social identity and only secondly as individual people with their own thoughts, desires, and convictions. The relationship between "collective identities" and "personal sexual agency" in the case of race play performed by racialized women is highlighted. Each time a racialized woman engages in a BDSM performance, it is perceived as race play. This is also the remark of Jordi who identifies himself as a slave. On apps like Growlr and Scruff, "Please dominate/fuck me" is not an uncommon introductory message that he received from many white women and men who explicitly state that they want to be completely used by my "big black cock." As he mentions, the causes of this identification are historical:

> The stereotype of the massively endowed black brute with insatiable and animalistic sexual urges dates back to the Trans-Atlantic slavery. Black men were seen as brutal, aggressive and strong, and therefore, useful when it came to hard labor. But black men were also sold with a huge caution label – one that painted them as dangerous. The fear was that this big black brute is strong and useful, but would also probably attempt to rape your entire family if given the chance.

According to him, it is common to meet white people who do not desire him completely for what he is, but rather he is conscious of "being pursued or desired as a checklist of traits (namely, a big black cock) that feed urges rooted in racial fetishization".

> These fetishizing urges never died, but have followed us into this century. For many Jewish people and non-whites, being asked to dominate a white person feels like fetishization, and being asked to submit to a white person feels like actual slavery/anti-semitism. It makes some people uncomfortable, and for very valid reasons.

In these settings of power imbalance alongside infliction of sexual violence on their money slaves, "their race becomes the defining feature of the BDSM-scene as well." "This brings to light the assumed neutrality of white people, where a person of color will always necessarily 'perform race' in a BDSM play" (Shotanus 2017).

In order for Taoufik to feel enjoyment, the dimension of the mistress's revenge must be operative. In an enemy ethnic group, Taoufik literally has to feel that "they want to make him pay." The colonialist hierarchy is here reversed: the Arab woman subjugates the white man.

How does this inversion work? It seems that the assimilation of the submissive to the whore is at the heart of the fantasy scenario. Messages from neighborhood dominas are rife with insults, transforming the submissive man into, precisely, a "white whore". Thus, like money, the discourse of racial and gender hatred (exemplified by the expression "white whores") is also part of the libidinal foundations of these "scum" practices. As a lure, humiliation would then have a similar function to the pleasure that the money mistress is supposed to take: to help men convince themselves that the women whose erotic performance they consume (in the form of pornography or money) also find their enjoyment in it – not only for its financial aspects but also on a libidinal level. It seems that this illusion of symmetry or fair exchange is necessary for sexual enjoyment to be possible. I speak of illusion because, independently of the fact that the women involved do enjoy, on all other levels, the asymmetrical nature of the economic-sexual relationship cannot be denied.

Taoufik's fantasy of financial slavery also fully subscribes to the split described by Freud (1924) between mother and whore, where sexuality and affection are experienced in different spheres and with different partners. Taoufik rationalizes this split on the basis of the alleged ontological difference between men and women in terms of erotic economy and desire, thus justifying his desire for women with whom he does not want to have a relationship.

> Taoufik: I think that when women enjoy being with a man, they really appreciate him for who he is, they have feelings, I'm speaking in a general sense. On the contrary, men are more interested in physical attractiveness. So, as a man, I don't really need someone intelligent in order to be excited. For me, intelligence is separate from that.

This explains the reference to money mistresses being bitches and the frequent critical description of their bodies. On the one hand, in their own social circle, in front of their friends in a context where their masculinity should be recognized, young white men (or men who identify as such in the fantasy) can reverse this power relationship by humiliating these women publicly by sharing screenshots of conversations on their wall.

On the other hand, the fragile reversal of power and hierarchy can at any time be interrupted by a sudden return to order. Even though the money mistresses may call these men "whores," they are at all times likely to be called by the same adjective, and much more easily, because they are, de facto, women paid for a sexual service. The humiliation only works insofar as the clients agree to play along. At the slightest misstep, bad taste, or miscalculation or simply when the man gets bored, the dominant woman is returned to her status of abjection. Ultimately, the gender diss responds to economic and social class inequality and power hierarchy.

4.8 Between guilt, humiliation, and enjoyment: on a slight slope of dependence

In financial slavery as Taoufik experiences it, shame intensifies pleasure, and we may wonder whether his masochism is not in itself a defense meant to overcome the contradictions of a masculinity experienced as both privileged and discredited.

Taoufik's masculinity is discredited and then excluded from hegemonic masculinity mainly because he is a non-white man living and working in Paris, coming from an ex-colony of France and because he enjoys being submissive, being "played" by a woman, which means assuming a position contrary to virile masculinity[9] whose psychological mechanism is underpinned by the shame of being mistaken for a woman (Molinier 2000).

In the case of money slaves, the shame and abject status of being treated as "a whore" is eroticized. Presumably, the shame of lacking manhood first caused suffering: Jacques Brunet-Georget (2009) speaks of the "painful individuation" caused by the shame of being excluded from hegemonic masculinity or of not being able to identify with it because of one's bottom sexuality.

However, if Taoufik has eroticized the shame of not being part of hegemonic masculinity, Taoufik's case suggests that a white, masculine, privileged man is far from absent from his fantasy of humiliation, which is inextricably linked to his fantasy of being dominated as a white man (and thus enjoying the humiliation of whites) and the way he interprets North African women's involvement in these practices. The remarkable profitability of male hegemony allows Taoufik to belong to a masculinity torn between the hegemonic ideal and a minority status, and to enjoy its arbitrary premium, the patriarchal dividend: paying to enjoy the bodies of others, "buying" and thus consuming female bodies, and/or possibly proving to himself that he has power over them via money.

However, Taoufik also adds another dimension, by referring to his objective guilt, as a man who feels he is benefiting from the "dividends of patriarchy."

> I was raised in a wealthy family in a poor country. I've seen terrible poverty and yet I grew up in comfort. There is a kind of social guilt that I've felt and that might explain my need to give to those I imagine as poor because I'm conscious of how lucky I've been. Another thing is that I was made very aware, in my family, of the violence committed against women and so there is perhaps a form of guilt that I want to compensate for.

The mention of Taoufik's social guilt toward other Moroccans (and, by extension, toward other non-whites and ex-colonized people) because of his privileged economic status, which makes him similar to whites, and toward women, because as a man he belongs to the oppressor group, suggests a link between guilt, humiliation, and pleasure. This guilt evokes the anxiety of being assimilated, by Moroccans, to the social enemy – the white man. Financial slavery would thus represent a space where his sexuality – which brings him disturbingly close to hegemonic masculinity, because of the objectification of female bodies that operates there – can be assumed, while sparing him this class, gendered, and postcolonial anguish. This guilt is, in fact, suspended, canceled, or diverted by the humiliation inflicted on him by the women he pays. However, the suspension of this guilt leads Taoufik into an increasingly costly race. Indeed, what is striking about this practice is the role of the amount of money spent in the pleasure taken. In this regard, Taoufik acknowledged that sexual enjoyment depends essentially on the money spent:

> At the moment I pretty much need venal domination in order to be turned on. I could even go further, in the sense that in the beginning, the first few times I paid, I was paying for a service, while today I no longer pay for a service in order to be dominated, today it's the fact of paying itself that is a source of mental and sexual pleasure. ... For years, I have been going back and forth between times when I realize, when I tell myself that this can't continue, and times when I've been good and things are better and then, I fall back into it. I've been in therapy for years. I've been to different therapists, different addiction centers.

Taoufik speaks about his relationship to *money slavering* as a form of addiction. The road toward repetition compulsion can prove dangerous: the enjoyment of spending means that the sums invested are increasing. After having gotten himself into a "financially catastrophic situation", Taoufik has had to sell his car. Here we could appreciate a way that financial slavery turns what I see as a kind of psychic retreat from social guilt into a space of dependence tightening the vise of social identities – gender, sexual, racial.

The problem is that the sexual drives do not meet a strict limit. The death drive most of the time in those practices does not meet a flesh and blood interlocutor who could help to re-establish the cleavage. Thus, it can make it harder for practitioners to work their sexual drives in a way that is conducive to the care and preservation of the health of everyone involved. The insufficiency of support of the sexual excitation does not give to the adult sufficient feelings of safety so that it engages in a relation of safety and trust. This can be put in perspective with the notion of the "I-Skin" of Didier Anzieu. Ego-Skin finds its support on the three functions of the skin: a link and a primary means of exchange with others, a surface that marks the limit with the outside, and a bag that retains inside.

> There is a need for the psychic apparatus, whether it is individual or group, to constitute an envelope which contains it, which delimits it, which protects it and which allows exchanges with the outside, that is to say a skin-Ego.
>
> *(Anzieu 1985)*

It should be noted that these practices involve women who are sometimes very young, sometimes acting in groups, and sometimes under the age of majority. It is therefore necessary to take into account the role of the feeling of impunity and the role of emulation that the Internet supports and reinforces.

4.9 Discussion

This analysis of online sexual fantasy makes me think that we need to revisit traditional psychoanalytic concepts such as personal identity and fantasy within the framework of this new reality so that we may appreciate how online experience does and doesn't facilitate the formation of subjectivity and diversity. This is particularly important given that as the coronavirus continues to spread globally, social distancing, self-isolation/quarantine, and national lockdowns have become the cores to control the pandemic (Zhang and Ma). Analysis of sex work and COVID-19 guidelines published by five community-based organizations found that they focused on altering sexual practices, enhancing hygiene, and pivoting to virtual work (Callander et al. 2020). That's the case of Amelie who started to develop interest in virtual domination as she had to close her shop during the lockdown and discovered she could make money out of female domination as she was broke.

Thanks to the virtual space, women can enjoy subverting the gender and race relationship by expressing the desire they wouldn't usually be allowed to express while earning pocket money without having to leave their room and while, as Amelie told me, they don't have to touch them, see them, or smell them.

Teela Sanders (2005) argued already in her article on sex worker strategies that BDSM is the easy way of making a better profit on sex work as BDSM services are better paid. Nonetheless, this economical motivation of money mistresses is frequently represented by the (white) mainstream BDSM community as if it was their unique interest in that activity, representing them as mere predators abusing vulnerable men, as well as impostors spreading a false idea of what BDSM should be. This depiction was contradicted by interviews with field observations of and other data about money mistresses and other dominant women, which rather suggests that there is a taboo of money within that BDSM community. This taboo may be used as a distinction strategy by dominant white women as a defense to protect themselves against the whore stigma, promote their own *bourgeois* dominant status, and at the same time, disqualify and marginalize the practices of racialized, lower-class women, based on the money exchanges they involve.

In fact, one message the interviewed money mistresses communicated clearly is that they are not driven solely by simple economic exigency. Instead, they are also searching for pleasure in relations where they find respect, and more specifically, in the money slavery "game" that involves a pleasurable inversion of traditional gender and race relationships, and a money exchange that is *also* highly eroticized. On the contrary, the idea that certain women of "migrant origins" use sexuality to abusively benefit from their white male partners' money is a classical postcolonial stereotype (Charsley and Benson 2012). However, what is new is the emergence, in the form of *money slavering*, of a new possibility: for men not to suffer but enjoy this male fantasy pattern, and for women, if not to enjoy it – which, unless proven otherwise, remains a possibility – then at least exploit it economically. This possibility was already inherent in the relationship between an older man (a *sugar daddy*) and a young woman (a *sugar baby*), who would receive material compensation for her time, presence, and sexual services. The new element of *money slavering* is the reclaiming of these practices by young women.[10] This is what is new in this practice: the emergence of a new possibility for women to enjoy this scenario both libidinally and economically, as humorously expressed by the singer Yeliz in her song "Où sont mes boloss" (2010).

Accordingly, the money mistresses' risk of being violently insulted during their online practices is present and serious. Men who enjoy being debased and spending excessively while conjuring their masochism occasionally redirect the flow of (racial) hatred back to its female sender. Thus, the fantasies involved in money slavering overflow the fixity of social identities of gender, sex, race, and class, through subjectivity, but *money slavering* also contains the conditions of a movement in and out of these social orders, causing a twisting and revealing of their insides as simultaneously dehumanizing and fragile – Mobius strip style.

The interpretations put forward by Geoff Mains (1984) and Robert Hopcke (1991), for whom male submission is a kind of catharsis for men overwhelmed by the "tensions of social competition," appear invalid for men performing money slavering. According to Mistress K.

> [O]ften it's people who don't have a big salary who are in these practices. I don't understand how it happens, but often, the less they earn, the more they spend of their salary. But often it's their choice to live like that, the one who is going to earn 8,000/10,000 € will give you 2,000 € maximum, [but when] he earns 1,100 €, well …. 900 € go in my pocket, and I didn't ask for

anything, it's just them who want to impress us, but as we don't play their games, in general they continue and are even very happy with this choice of life, it's their fantasy. A money slave is not necessarily rich but just aware that 80% of his money points to his money mistress .... Deprivation is the secret of a true money slave.

It seems that the commitment to meaningful work threatens to limit the dependence to these practices. K. mentions that she has not become addicted to these practices because she works on the side and is in a relationship. This helps her "keep her feet on the ground" and keep in mind that "it's just a game." "Not all men are submissive. She is not just dominant." She says that this line between reality and play may be harder to maintain because some 16- to 20-year-old girls fall into this trap because they can earn astronomical amounts of money in ten minutes.

If we are to formulate a hypothesis related to the concept of suffering at work, I believe that it is not in terms of overwork but rather around conjuring the ever-present risk of the capitalist market: either being played by or playing the other, specifically by selling useless products or inexistent services; in other words, lies. This is the daily bread of neoliberal competition, including all its symptomatic avatars such as fakes and bullshit jobs[11] (Graeber 2018: 38), of which financial slavery would represent one libidinal mechanism.

Thus, the principles, norms, and rules operating in the field of work have the capacity not only to affect fantasies but also to constitute them. Because we learn to desire within the capitalist economy, the latter remains the engine of desire. In this regard, Linda Williams (1991) has seen the money shot (a pornographic image of a penis engorged repeatedly in order to ejaculate) as a distillation of all the principles of late capitalism aimed at consumer pleasure. The fantasy of money slavery seems to me typical of neoliberalism, insofar as the submissives are excited by the very idea of being "ripped off." I argue that this fantasy represents one libidinal mechanism of neoliberalism. This chapter shows that it's caught up in a highly specific structuring of social relations in terms of gender, class, and race.

Notes

1 Translator's note: While the term "financial slavery" is much more common on the English-speaking web, I have decided to retain the French neologism "money slavering," which is specific to the context of this study.
2 G. Rubin, speech given at the ceremony for the Journey man II Academy on October 4, 1997 (Weiss 2011: 6).
3 Translator's note: *Racaille* has been translated as "trash," "scum," or "rabble," but its stigmatizing and ambivalent nature isn't quite captured by any of these English equivalents. Although historically applied to different groups rejected by the mainstream society, in recent years *racaille* has come to denote, almost exclusively, young people of mostly African origin living in suburban estates and associated by the right-wing media with delinquency or crime. At the same time, it has sometimes been reclaimed by different marginalized populations and used positively to denote a personal style.

4 The concept of subaltern is a milestone to the Spivak theory. The "subaltern" is a military term which means "of lower rank." The term is borrowed from Italian Marxist Antonio Gramsci. In her essay "Can the Subaltern Speak?" Spivak (1988, 1993) exposes the irony that the subalterns have awakened to a consciousness of their own rights by making practical utterances against unjust domination and inequality. She denounces the harm done to women/third world women and non-Europeans to be represented as objects we are talking about but who cannot speak for themselves or who are silent. She attacks the Eurocentric attitudes of the West. She holds that knowledge is never innocent. The knowledge about the third world is always constructed with the political and economic interests of the West.

5 See the concept of the eccentric subject by Teresa de Lauretis in "Eccentric Subjects: Feminist Theory and Historical Consciousness" (de Lauretis 1990).

6 The concept of hegemonic masculinity allows to "take into account the structural inequalities" while imagining masculinities and femininities as a "configuration of practices" carried out within social practices (Connell and Messerschmidt 2005). According to Connell, hegemonic masculinity is implanted in the subjectivity of each man and woman. It differs from the real activities or relationships of most men or women and instead represents a social ideal that men strive to attain and that is allegedly desirable to women. Hegemonic masculinity can only be grasped relationally; in other words, its reproduction is dependent on other masculinities – complicit (aspiring to hegemonic masculinity without fully reaching it), subordinate (excluded from hegemonic masculinity through the practice of non-normative sexualities), or marginalized (excluded by certain factors such as origin or skin color) – and on the different femininities that either consolidate or reject it.

7 Translator's note: The mistress's name is a pun on *Moroccan Queen* and *haine*, hatred.

8 Ariane Cruz's *The Color of Kink* (2016) is the first monograph on race play. Cruz explores black women's representations and performances within American pornography and BDSM from the 1930s to the present.

9 By virility, I mean a defense collectively constructed by men in spaces of masculine sociability (specifically at work) in order to fight against fear and vulnerability, which allows them to ground their privileges in self-control. Proving one's virility by denying one's vulnerability is a condition of belonging to the dominant group.

10 We find a humorous version of this reclaiming in the song "Où sont mes boloss" ["Where Are My Losers"] by Yeliz (2010), *Dailymotion*, https://www.dailymotion.com/video/xf4255

11 Graeber defines it as "useless or dangerous activities which usually also involve some degree of pretense and lies."

Bibliography

Altman D. (2001). *Global Sex*. Chicago, IL, The University of Chicago Press.

Anzieu D. (1985). *Le moi-peau*. Malakoff, Dunod.

Baatz U. (1993). Das Spiel ist ernst, der Ernst ist Spiel. In U. Baatz, W. Müller-Funk (Hrsg.), *Vom Ernst des Spiels*. Über Spiel und Spieltheorie, 5–20. Berlin, Dietrich Reimer Verlag.

Brunet-Georget J. (2009). La honte au corps: vers le réel de la performance S/M. Genre, sexualité & société [online], 2. http://journals.openedition.org/gss/1024; https://doi.org/10.4000/gss.1024

Callander D., Meunier É., Deveau R., Grov C., Donovan B., Minichiello V., Singham Goodwin A., Duncan D. T. (2020). Sex workers are returning to work and require enhanced support in the face of COVID-19: Results from a longitudinal analysis of online sex work activity and a content analysis of safer sex work guidelines. *Sexual Health*, 17(4), 384–386. https://doi.org/10.1071/SH20128

Charsley K., Benson M. C. (2012). Marriages of convenience or inconvenient marriages: regulating spousal migration to Britain. *Journal of Immigration, Asylum and Nationality Law*, 26(1), 10–26.

Connell R., Messerschmidt J. (2005). Hegemonic Masculinity: Rethinking the Concept. *Gender and Society*, 19(6), 829–855.

Cruz A. (2016) *The Color of Kink: Black Women, BDSM, and Pornography*. New York, NYU Press.

De Lauretis T. (1990). Eccentric Subjects: Feminist Theory and Historical Consciousness [en ligne]. *Feminist Studies*, 16(1), Spring, 115–150. Disponible.

Freud S. (1924). *Ma vie et la psychanalyse*. Paris, Gallimard.

Goffman E. (1959). *The Presentation of Self in Everyday Life*. New York, Doubleday.

Graeber D. (2018). *Bullshit Jobs*. New York, Klett.

Hopcke R. (1991). S/M and the psychology of male initiation: An archetypal perspective. In M. Thompson (Ed.), *Leatherfolk: Radical Sex, People, Politics, and Practice*. Boston, MA: Alyson Books.

Levey T., Pinsky D. (2015a). A constellation of stigmas: intersectional stigma management and the professional dominatrix. *Deviant Behavior*, 36(5), 347–367.

Levey T. G., Pinsky D. (2015b). 'A world turned upside down': Emotional labour and the professional dominatrix. *Sexualities*, 18(4), 438–458.

Lugand N. (2017). La domination féminine dans la sexualité BDSM hétérosexuelle. PhD diss., Université Paris 13 Sorbonne nord.

Lugand N., Molinier P., Billand J. (Forthcoming). Dominas de quartier et pigeons: une approche intersectionnelle du *money slavering* « en mode racaille » sur Facebook. In S. Cromer, C. Passard (Eds.), *Les usages sociaux de l'insulte*. Paris, PUF.

Mains G. (1984). *Urban Aboriginals: A Celebration of Leathersexuality*. San Francisco, CA, Gay Sunshine Press.

Miller P., Devon M. (1995). *Screw the Roses, Send Me the Thorn: The Romance and Sexual Sorcery of Sadomasochism*. Fairfield, CT, Mystic Roses Books.

Molinier P. (2000). Virilité défensive, masculinité créatrice. *Travail, genre et sociétés*, 3(1), 25–44.

Molinier P. (2006). *Les enjeux psychiques du travail*. Paris, Petite Bibliothèque Payot.

Molinier P., Laugier S., Paperman P. (2009). *Qu'est-ce que le care. Souci des autres, sensibilité, responsabilité*. Paris, Petite Bibliothèque Payot.

Moser C., Madeson J. (2002). *Bound to Be Free: The SM Experience*. New York, Continuum.

Musser A. J. (2014). *Sensational Flesch: Race, Power and Masochism*. New York, University Press.

Pheterson G. (2001). *Le prisme de la prostitution*. Paris, l'Harmattan, Bibliothèque du féminisme.

Puaud D. (2012). De la condition ouvrière à la condition racaille: Entre assignation identitaire et actes de résistances. LMSI.net, 2 Juin 2012. http://lmsi.net/De-la-condition-ouvriere-a-la

Sanders T. (2005). 'It's just acting': Sex workers' strategies for capitalizing on sexuality. *Gender Work and Organization*, 12(4), 319–342.

Scott G. G. (1997). *Erotic Power: An Exploration of Dominance and Submission*. Secaucus, NJ, Citadel.

Shotanus M. S. (2017). Racism or race play: A conceptual investigation of the race play debates. *Zapruder World* [online], 4, 22.

Spivak, G. C. (1988). Can the Subaltern Speak? In C. Nelson, L. Grossberg (Eds.), *Marxism and the Interpretation of Culture*. London: Macmillan.

Spivak G. C. (1993). Can the subaltern speak? Reprinted in P. Williams, L. Christman (Eds.), *Colonial Discourse and Post-colonial Theory*. Coleshill: Harvester Wheatsheaf.

Vogl J. (2013). *Le spectre du capital*. Paris, Diaphanes.

Weiss M. (2011). *Techniques of Pleasure: BDSM and the Circuits of Sexuality*. Durham, NC, Duke University Press.

Wetzstein T. A., Steinmetz L., Reis C., Eckert R. (1993). *Sadomasochismus Szenen und Rituale*. Hamburg, Rowohlt Tachenbuch Verlag.

Williams L. (1991). *Hardcore: Power, Pleasure and the Frenzy of the Visible*. London, Pandora Press.

Wiseman J. (1996). *SM 101: A Realistic Introduction*. Emeryville, CA, Greenery Press.

Yeliz. (2010). "Où sont mes boloss." https://www.youtube.com/watch?v=BC6SDvE-KTA

Zhang Y., Ma Z. F. (2020). Impact of the COVID-19 pandemic on mental health and quality of life among local residents in Liaoning Province, China: A cross-sectional study. *International Journal of Environmental Research and Public Health*, 17(7), 2381. https://doi.org/10.3390/ijerph17072381. PMID: 32244498; PMCID: PMC7177660

5

CONCLUSION

5.1 Separation between professional and non-professional domination: a scam

I can say that my study of female domination has been a real adventure. It is an adventure because I started with my preconceived ideas, beliefs, and assertions, which very quickly made me stumble along the way. Surprised by difficulties that I had not been able to anticipate, both professionally and in my private life, I had to seriously question myself in order to get back up and change direction, or even turn around, guided by significant people who gave me the will to pursue this research object. Ultimately, I discovered something totally different from what I was originally looking for. In this regard, my immersion with professional dominatrixes was the experience that marked me, and on which I reflected the most.

In this productive experience, the role of the body and of core sensations for intuitive knowledge is very important. Indeed, it constitutes a matrix on which my theoretical material is built. By breaking the taboo of the prostitute and prostitution, I exposed myself directly to the whore stigma. I thus pushed my body into a painful experience. This sensation that ran through my body was the source of my awareness of the links between professional and non-professional practices of female domination. This is how I began to notice what is lost by erasing these links.

By listening to the stories of each of them and their lived adventures in relation to female domination, I realized that all practitioners owe a debt to professional dominatrixes. Against the ideal of the sexual double standard, which animates some discourses on sexuality, by giving voice back to the individual sensibilities of professional dominatrixes and their maintenance, one becomes aware of the dependence on their experience and perspective to call themselves dominant and submissive.

DOI: 10.4324/9781003258537-7

First of all, as I have shown in Chapter 1, the experiences of professional dominatrixes, related in initiation guides to female domination, serve as a guide to all practitioners of female domination. On the other hand, the men interviewed have had many paid relationships with professional dominatrixes. Many submissives begin their BDSM careers with professional dominatrixes, so to speak. Thus they can begin to learn about female domination in the places where techniques and practices with professionals are initiated. If, in this context, they let the dominatrix lead, when they address a non-professional woman, they will have gained experience and will be better able to judge their partners by comparing them, based on their experience, to professional dominatrixes. At the same time that some submissives are critical of professional dominatrixes, especially in terms of their financial interest in these relationships, submissives rely on these experiences as reference points in their sexuality. Awareness of the connections between professional and non-professional female domination highlights how the sexual double standard benefits them. They are able to accumulate experience and knowledge about the practices of female domination quickly as they are better able than women to navigate the two spheres of female domination (professional and non-professional) unaffected by the whore stigma.

Also, if a double standard is present, as some of the comments made by semi-professional dominatrixes justifying their relationship with money attest (see Chapter 4), there are also defectors and transitional spaces. Some dominatrixes practice professionally and also for pleasure. I add for my part that there is a real entanglement between professional and non-professional sexuality. It is possible to move from a form of exchange of sexual services for material compensation to a form of exchange of sexual services not involving material compensation with the same person; a woman can offer professional dominatrix services and be dominant in her private life. Similarly, non-professional dominatrixes draw on each other's practices, such as session organization, usage formulas and wish lists. The greetings and courtesies in a relationship between a submissive and a dominatrix, certain rules for organizing sessions, the use of certain tools such as wish lists in communication with the submissive are similar to both forms of female domination practices for example.

I emphasize that certain skills developed in the context of these practices, such as the importance of working with boundaries (see Chapter 2), are not only common to professional and non-professional dominatrixes, but common to all women working in an activity whose function is dedicated to a global mission of care.

Thus to think of venal and non-venal female domination separately would be to ignore the multiplicity of relations that unite them: these relations concern the persons, the modalities of the relations, and the economic aspect of the latter (see Tabet 2004).

These connections are present everywhere in BDSM communities. Non-commercial female domination therefore does not negate commercial female domination. Commercial female domination is the other term for the relationships of non-commercial female domination. If the links between commercial and non-commercial female domination are hidden and illegitimate, they are nonetheless interesting, useful and even indispensable.

5.2 A logic of separation that touches the unconscious: the role of the whore stigma

The weight of sexual morality has led to the erasure of despised bodies of prostitutes, because of their vocation to give pleasure in exchange for a retribution. As I have shown the lack of attention paid to relationships involving professional dominatrixes, the lack of perception of the importance that people give to their experience is largely due to the role of the whore stigma, an instrument at the service of the sexual morality. The whore disturbs the established order, which is patriarchal but, of course, heterosexual, and the white supremacy that directs the plot too. That is because the whore stigma is the cog in the wheel of not only women's oppression but also homophobic and racial oppression, as Chapter 4 demonstrates. Prostitution is the other side of sexual morality, and the body of the whore is the cursed place where the Other is rejected in an absolute way. It is not surprising, then, that the whore stigma plays such an important role in the discovery of our erotic body and our sexuality. I affirm that the shame of the association to the figure of the whore is part of the fundamental sufferings to which the bodies of all women are confronted. This suffering would be caused by the shame of being excluded or rejected from the category of the good woman, and of not being able to identify with the latter because of the expression of her erotic body. Thus, the body encounters its limits, the limit of its possibilities that is imposed on it. This is how women experience their own body, their power to act, by experiencing suffering. This sensation of shame lived in the prism of the whore stigma feeds and structures the subjectivation. The whore stigma is part of the unconscious biases that influence the process of interacting with others. Understanding these processes requires a psychodynamic frame of reference which mobilized the concepts of psychic suffering, the unconscious, and defense.

5.3 Defenses against the whore stigma or working to becoming a naturally dominant woman

Since we have learned to desire within a form of social organization that stigmatizes prostitutes, the logic of this system acts from desire. It is through this figure of the whore, in the negative therefore, that the sexual identity of the dominant woman is constructed. All that the dominant woman expels from her strong interior is projected on the body of the whore: the cursed place where the other is pushed back in an absolute way. The discovery of the dominant woman's personality is ordered by a negative syntactic and categorical structure, a structure of self-hatred.

Thus, dominant women define themselves by distinguishing themselves from what they are not. Thus, the discovery of her dominant personality depends on the characteristics that distinguish her from the common, the vulgar, and the low class with which the whore is associated. I see the strategies adopted in the process of creating the dominant personality as a defense in response to the whore stigma.

As a matter of fact, dominant women distinguish themselves from the figure of the whore by showing arrogance, beauty, exception, class, elegance in the style of dress, the finesse of oral or written expression, or by a marked disinterest in money.

They would naturally be so, since they are always dominant. However, all those notions are themselves dependent on the management of bodily distances. In the management of the body work there is work of the limits (see Chapter 2). Indeed, the body of the dominatrix is an object of work, whether it is commercial or non-commercial female domination. In their performance as dominant woman it is the body which is vector of an ideal of the dominatrix. In general, in many accounts of female domination, this control of bodily distances represents one of the main aspects of the dominatrix. It is only under the constraint of having to set limits with men that the disposition to master, control, and dominate men has any chance of developing.

In short, one is not born dominant, but becomes dominant. A *naturally* dominant woman as submissives seek and these women define themselves is an oxymoron. The experience of work transforms the subject, and we cannot do without it to think about the psychological processes that we attribute to the personality or sexual identity of subjects (Molinier et al. 2009: 17). However, if this strategy involved in the process of creating a dominant personality is the result of hard work, effort is denied. By defining themselves as *naturally* dominant, women support a perspective of the subject that precedes work by showing that the body of desire, the body of pleasure, and the erogenous body have been inherited from innate dispositions rather than from relationships with parents, friends, and relatives (Dejours 2001: 73). The argument of naturalness is used as a defense by many of the women interviewed. To the question "What were/are your first fantasies related to female domination, desire, fetishes, etc.?" most of the women I interviewed did not answer, but instead they circumvented it by justifying that there is a continuity between the personality and the passive or active sexual orientation. The strength of character, the spirit of initiative, and the spirit of rebellion, which are already present in childhood, are invoked to explain "naturally" their sexual orientations. Thus, some women practicing female domination think that taking charge and directing everything is part of their nature, certainly a dominant nature. Knowing the risks faced by women when talking about their sexuality, especially when their sexuality moves away from the "good sexuality," I interpret their attitude as a defense to protect themselves from the risk linked to the stigma of the whore.

The problem is that this reference to naturalness invisibilizes the fantasies, desires and pleasures associated with female dominance and at the same time supports the prejudice that men have stronger sexual drives than women.

This defense is thus inscribed in the process of muliebrity and subordinated to the defensive interests of virility. One can notice certain consequences of those strategies and behaviors: crushing responsibility for the dominatrix, tensions between sometimes contradictory requirements, fear of insults and judgments, tiredness related to the attention required and decentered toward others, and lack of time to take care of oneself and to nourish one's own dreams, one's own hopes, one's own desires, one's own fantasies, and one's own sensuality.

The speech of the dominant women brings a touch of youth to this ethic of selfless love, of the gift of the mothers to their children. Yet, according to Haraway's formula, there are narratives that can seriously damage health. A narrative that is largely ignorant of sexuality, ignorant of attachment, ignorant of the knowledge of bare hands, ignorant of the reality of work, and ignorant of the complexity of moral perception in situations is seriously damaging to women's health and dignity (Haraway 1991).

5.4 A logic that touches the heart of our sexual fantasies: the subversion of the whore stigma and the stigma of prostitution and its limits

Understanding that sexual morality is not a force imposed on us from outside but that our subjectivities are involved and play a role in its functioning implies recognizing that domination is implanted in the very heart of fantasy – the thread of infantile neurosis is inextricably woven with that of the social.

This fantasy of being a whore and the fantasy of prostitution are important cogs in masochistic fantasies where the process of submission is activated by the shame of identifying with the fallen woman (Lugand 2017). And by mobilizing the body, "the effect of shame intensifies and/or renews the exploration of sexual pleasure[1]" (Hart 2003). The fantasy of the whore generates a disturbance of the submissive's sexual identity, a discomfort, a shame, even a feeling of anguish from which he can work on the enigma that he is. It is through the sensations of this bound, bruised, battered body – a scarred skin – as Didier Anzieu would say, that the movement of thought can be initiated (Dejours 2001: 150). A movement that allows the submissive to grasp in the behavior of others precious elements of a knowledge of himself otherwise inaccessible, elements that could allow him to question the sexual morality.

However, the destiny of the movement of thought, motor of the transformation of oneself and of our relationships, is itself dependent on the capacity to see in the fallen women a precious source of clues for the understanding of our own unconscious elaborations. It is only on this condition that an overcoming of the violence proper to this form of social organization experienced through the prism of the whore stigma – sensitive especially in intimate relations – seems to be possible. The cases of the masochist M. studied by Michel De M'Uzan (1997) and the case of Sacher-Masoch described by Wanda von Sacher-Masoch (2014) show, indeed, that an identification with the figure of the whore – whose conduct is faulty – is painful and prevents the relationship to the Other. Sacher-Masoch and M. defend themselves from this identification with the women occasioned by the practice of a masochist sexuality. Indeed, Sacher-Masoch judges immoral all women who would come too close to his fantasy and separates from them, while M. reiterates the sexual morality by failing to maintain a conjugal relationship with a prostitute judged dishonest in her sexual practice. The distancing from prostitutes is correlative in his case to the cleavage established between the perverse domain and the decent family life (Lugand and Molinier 2017). The sexual practices carry then the bodies and the beings in an experience where the violence, the suffering, and the humiliation exclude the tenderness, the complicity, and the concern of the other. The memory of the pleasure felt from the experience of masochism is marked by the shadow of guilt. When the threat of the stigma of homophobia was revealed as blatant, all that remained for Sacher-Masoch was to eradicate it in an act of self-defense, paralyzed by a feeling of shame by whipping their play partner with the whore stigma in order for their male partners to reconstitute their narcissism. The shame of the identification with the figure of the fallen woman generates a trouble in the gender elusive, which remains unjustifiable in itself.

The idealization of the phantasmatic mother at the heart of the gynarchic fantasies can also be interpreted as a defense intrinsically linked to the guilt incorporated in the subjectivity of men in order to thwart their desires and fantasies of submission. The fantasy of prostitution in terms of forced sex trafficking is addressed by many gynarchists including Luc. The latter has the fantasy of being a young boy emigrating to a gynarchist country sold by his mother on a market for "naive" untrained young men. "Some women are willing to pay to have one trained." So the rules of our kinship system not only influence our fantasies but also constitute elements organizing certain fantasies.

Thus, the gynarchists not being able to affirm their desire of a sexuality, which transgresses the limits and represents "a dangerous threat of pollution for the social system synecdochically represented by the body" (Butler 1990), must disguise it under the features of an idealized love. Yet, as I have shown, the danger of the idealization of the object is the loss of the sense of reality and the neglect of the limits of psychic tolerance of their play partner who is getting worse and worse. The other becomes intrusive in relation to his own body.

In these cases, there is a continuum between shame and guilt experienced through the prism of the male defense of virility. It highlights men's anxiety about a sexuality where they will be submissive to women. The defenses around shame block the ability to engage with the world. Pushed to their limits, they confront us with an otherness that is not only traumatized but also traumatizing (De Greef 1994).

The question arises as to whether the decisive character of the violence experienced and expressed comes from a simple disappointment in relation to what was expected or whether it is due to a conflict between internal forces that necessarily – and often repeatedly – bring us back into the proximity of certain dangers. It, thus, appears that the fantasy of the whore and of prostitution struggles on several levels where it cannot be integrated, generating a tension. This fantasy is de facto in tension with the social requirement of conformity with virility, valued in many male jobs.

Here, what is considered shameful, unworthy of a man, is to be unable to control the masochistic tendency of his own sexual drives, to express his narcissism, to abandon himself, to find pleasure in the abdication of power.

The tensions felt and the violence expressed allow us to understand the reversal that defensive virility operates in the register of values. The reference to virility makes it possible to anesthetize the moral sense (Molinier 2000). This confirms recent anthropological analyses (Ogilvie 2012) which have shown that the violence exercised toward others finds its source in the rejection of our condition as living beings, when this condition exhibits its contradictions and ambiguities. What we reject in others corresponds to what we refuse to recognize as our own. Violence can then be understood as an attempt to eliminate the part of the experience that the fantasy has elaborated in the night of the unconscious. An attempt to eliminate this experience in order to prevent it from intruding on conscious life and imposing itself in thought.

Those reactions of violence could also be related to the prohibition of certain games of the boy in childhood with his body. Those "amputations of the body" constitute, according to Dejours, the amential unconscious. Dejours distinguishes them from the repressed unconscious:

> They are registers of engagement of the child's body that have precisely been made impossible, that have been proscribed. But they are not proscribed for nothing; they were proscribed in a relation with the adult who, by his reactions, by prohibiting certain games of the body, prevented the child from appropriating his body. And when the child later on (big child, adolescent, adult) is brought back to these games, to these registers of engagement of the body which are proscribed, what he experiences is quite particular: it is not, as in the other registers, a question of a suffering; no, he experiences the collapse, the vertiginous fall in a void which, very quickly, takes the form of an anguish. It is an anguish that remains inaccessible to the therapy, manifesting itself in particular by somatizations and "passages to the act" which testify of an irrepressible endogenous and exogenous violence. Violence which expresses itself from the moment when we are unable to take charge of all the elements and the things which surround us, from the moment when there is a degradation of this knowledge and a loss of the sphere of the conditions of life.
>
> *(Dejours 2001)*

Like many authors who investigate BDSM practices, Hans van der Geest considers that in order to protect their mental equilibrium, the practitioners of these types of practices must be able to distinguish between their played performances and the relations of force in everyday life, to distance themselves from the relations of domination, and in short to be able to deconstruct for themselves what it is about the play and the violence in their relations (van der Geest 1990: 58). If we take seriously this principle at the heart of the BDSM ethic, we should take seriously the role of this stigma in female–dominated BDSM relationships as it hovers over the practitioners' drive destiny. The excessive violence of the emotions staged in S/M practices mobilizing the fantasy of whore or prostitution can go so far as to generate feelings of strangeness to oneself and generate violence in private life.

5.5 The choice to work together: another destiny for the whore stigma?

If the whore as a figure of otherness deserves a particular attention, it is because her intervention implies something other than the simple alternative between defense and subversion, namely empathy. It is possible to rediscover one's own body and the freedom to create meaning that is inherent in it. Bob Flanagan finds the strength to express his passion to a woman by exposing his bruised body, offering it to his dominatrix as her thing, and presenting himself as painslut, in a cultural and historical context dominated by the "male gaze" (Mulvey 1975). The public representation, the opening, is the place where the meeting between the self-representation of oneself and the recognition of the others is allowed. By objectifying his disabled male body, Flanagan would change the vision of male masochism. The reference to the supermasochist has a function of derision rather than admiration. It was through the experience of illness that Flanagan learned to combine suffering and sexual pleasure in a unique way, and he made it the substance of his artistic work and the main modality of his emotional and erotic life. The love relationship and the work, sometimes confused, sublimate the sadomasochistic experience of the disease. It is the passage to the work, thus the sublimation, which is the space of affirmation of oneself. Thanks to the work and to its recognition by the BDSM communities, it becomes then possible to assume a distance with the social implanted in oneself and to underline the political dimension that underlies the enterprise of self-representation. The sublimation as it requires the continuity of the process, thus, conjures the characteristics of the death drive to which it is charged to find an exit: repetition, compulsion, and violence were effectively sublimated by the creation.

What interests the communities, or what they face in their discussions, is not located at the level of masochistic or sadistic practices. Certainly it must deal with the fantasies, the desires, and the sexual tendencies which are in connection with the drives and at the origin of the investment in the BDSM communities. But it must especially work on the transformed expressions of the drives and of the framework, of the real circumstances in which they take shape. When the collective can be constituted in a common demand of reflexivity indexed on the reality, which is reflected in the dynamics of the deontic activity and of reflection on sexuality, it is then positive.

They are spaces where we are aware of relationships of domination and share a vision of sharing, an ethic that shapes our interaction. They are spaces where we can share our experiences and be "who we really are," spaces of justice and opportunity.

This positive aspect is limited by the collective defenses that also structure the life of the collective (Molinier 2006). It is then appropriate to consider the role of the whore stigma in the defensive dimensions at play in the practices while trying to ensure that the formation of stigma does not replay itself within these groups. The dangers of online sexual practices faced by some isolated practitioners of female domination suggest that BDSM relationships, defined by the absence of the collective, could become the ferment of a new form of gendered suffering and defense intertwined with ideologies of class and race. A paradigmatic post-modern figure of this rejected otherness: the "neighborhood dominas," young women, often of North African origin, present on social networks "mainly to make money," of popular class, represent the ideal type of the prostitute and are insulted as such.

The whore is a moral category, of course, but also a political one. An instrument of power that puts certain people aside, denigrates them, makes them invisible, and thus prevents us from realizing how much we are linked to each other.

In the practices of female domination, the importance of care, of the daily attention paid to others, is covered by the manifestations of sexuality, where the erotic body is given pride of place. The questions that work on this body and on us are essential because they echo the enigma that we are. When the chains of reciprocal erotic care can no longer unfold because each person is cut off from the memories he or she has of the relationships he or she has experienced, each person is cut off from his or her relationship to himself or herself and to his or her own erotic body. But sensitivity and memory participate in the deployment of an ethical attitude.

Thus, refusing to take into account professional domination because these relationships involve the transaction of money prevents the development of a new BDSM ethic that allows practitioners to nurture the erotic and moral values of mutual care and attention of the relationship. To refuse to recognize this link is to miss out on the sexual adventure, the one shared with the people we are in relationship with and the one that is our own.

Note

1 Lynda Hart tries to articulate shame and erotic interest in such a way that they allow for an intensification of pleasure by giving an ontological meaning to shame without reducing it to guilt (Hart 2003).

Bibliography

Anzieu D. (1985). *Le moi-peau*. Malakoff, Dunod.
Butler J. (1990). *Gender Trouble: Feminism and the Subversion of Identity*. New Yok, Routledge.
De Greef J. (1994). *"D'une substitution qui ne soit pas une usurpation."* Dans *Lévinas en contrastes, de M. Dupuis*, 51–64. Bruxelles, De Boeck Université.

De M'Uzan M. (1997). *De l'art à la mort*. Paris, Gallimard.

Dejours C. (2018). 2001. *Le corps d'abord*. Paris, Payot.

Haraway D. (1991). *Simians, Cyborgs and Women: The Reinvention of Nature*. New York, Routledge.

Hart L. (2003). *La Performance sadomasochiste: Entre Corps et Chair*. Paris, EPEL.

Lugand N. (2017). La domination féminine dans la sexualité BDSM hétérosexuelle. PhD diss., Université Paris 13 Sorbonne nord.

Lugand N., Molinier P. (2017). *Care et souci de soi dans les relations BDSM*. In M. Álvarez, I. Hekmat, S. Lauret (Eds.), *L'amour: Création et Société*. Paris, Michel Houdiard.

Molinier P. (2000). Virilité défensive, masculinité créatrice. *Travail, genre et sociétés*, 3(1), 25–44.

Molinier P. (2006). Le masochisme des femmes dans le travail: mythe sexiste ou défense professionnelle? Le cas des infirmières de bloc opératoire, *Psychologie clinique et projective*, 1(12), 211–230. www.cairn.info/revue-psychologie-clinique-et-projective-2006-1-page-211.htm. Consulté le 06/02/2022.

Molinier P., Laugier S., Paperman P. (2009). *Qu'est-ce que le care. Souci des autres, sensibilité, responsabilité*. Paris, Payot.

Mulvey L. (1975) Visual Pleasure and Narrative Cinema. *Screen*, 16(3), Autumn, 6–18. https://doi.org/10.1093/screen/1636

Ogilvie B. (2012). *L'homme jetable*. Paris, Editions Amsterdam.

Sacher-Masoch W. von (2014). *Confession de ma vie*. Paris, Rivages poche/Petite bibliothèque.

Tabet P. (2004). *La grande arnaque: Sexualité des femmes et échanges économico-sexuels*. Paris, L'Harmattan.

Van der Geest H. (1990). *Verschwiegene und abgelehnte Formen der Sexualität. Eine christliche Sicht*. Zürich, Theologischer Verlag.

Van der Geest H. (2003). Grenze und Ambivalenz. In T. Geisen, A. Karcher (Hrsg.), *Grenze: Sozial-politisch – Kulturell. Ambivalenz in den Prozessen der Entstehung und Veränderung von Grenzen*, 99–126. Frankfurt/M, IKO Verlag.

INDEX

Printed in the United States
by Baker & Taylor Publisher Services